EDUCATING OUR MASTERS

TO MY WIFE

Educating Our Masters

Influences on the growth of literacy in Victorian working class children

ALEC ELLIS
*Head of School of Librarianship
and Information Studies
Liverpool Polytechnic*

Gower

Published by Gower Publishing Company Limited, Gower House,
Croft Road, Aldershot, Hampshire GU11 3HR, England

and

Gower Publishing Company, Old Post Road,
Brookfield, Vermont 05036, U.S.A.

British Library Cataloguing in Publication Data

Ellis, Alec
   Educating our masters : influences on the growth of
   literacy in Victorian working class children.
   1. Literacy--Great Britain--History--19th century
   2. Labor and laboring classes--Education--Great Britain--
   History--19th century
   I. Title
   302.2'0941   LC156.G7

Library of Congress Cataloging in Publication Data

Ellis, Alec
   Educating our masters.

   Bibliography: p.
   Includes index.
   1. Labor and laboring classes--Education--Great Britain--
History--19th century. 2. Literacy--Great Britain--History--
19th century. 3. Labor and laboring classes--Great Britain--
Books and reading--History--19th century. 4. Children--Great
Britain--Books and reading--History--19th century. I. Title.
LC5056.G7E45 1985   371.96   85-7676

ISBN 0-566-00867-X

Printed by Paradigm Print,
Gateshead, Tyne and Wear

Contents

Preface

The Reform Bill of 1867 enfranchised the artisans
and other small householders, and whilst it fell
far short of the concept of universal manhood
suffrage, it nevertheless represented a genuine
move towards democratic government. On its passing
into law, Robert Lowe, until three years earlier
Vice President of the Committee of Council on
Education, suggested to the House of Commons his
belief that "it will be absolutely necessary that
you should prevail on our future masters to learn
their letters". His comment has since been popular-
ized as "We must educate our masters", and in this
book I have set out to examine many of the
influences on the growth of literacy in working
class children, not only since 1870, but throughout the Victorian period. My aim has been to
relate to the Victorian situation, the currently
accepted concepts of the conditions, social,
educational, and literary, which were likely to
foster or hinder the literacy of young people. The
term "working class" is intended to refer to the
children of independent manual workers, both
skilled and unskilled, but excludes the pauper
section of the community. It is appreciated that
many people were paupers at all times, and others
for varying periods during economic recessions,

but the intention has been to concentrate on their opportunities when they were not dependent on relief. It has not been possible to place the influences on literacy in any order of importance, for it is evident that all the factors are inter-related and would vary in importance from one child to another. However, although the difficul-ties with which children had to contend were great, it is apparent that having become regular in their attendance at school, the vast majority, certainly after 1860, was able to meet the educational standards required of it.

The present work was inspired by Richard D. Altick, who in his book The English Common Reader commented that "there is room for literally hundreds of studies of topics which are here merely sketched", and emphasized his desire "to provide a preliminary map of the vast territory, still virtually unexplored". Part of the material in Chapter 2 has appeared previously in The British Journal of Educational Studies (Volume 21, October 1973); part of that in Chapter 4 in an occasional publication of the History of Education Society entitled Victorian Education; and part of that in Chapter 8 in The Library Association Record (Volume 69, July 1967). The material in Chapter 6 has been dealt with in greater detail in the Library Association pamphlet, Books in Victor-ian Elementary Schools (1971). I am grateful to my publisher for giving me the opportunity to present the influences on the growth of literacy as a whole, for the parts already in print cannot but give an unbalanced view of the subject. In the decades when we are commemorating the various Elementary Education Acts of the 19th century, it seems fitting that the story should be told from this particular viewpoint, and perhaps move the reader to compare the situation which existed with that in our own time. Between 1870 and 1901 the found-ations of elementary and secondary education had been laid, and it is open to question whether the momentum of those years has been maintained in the present century.

Calderstones   ALEC ELLIS

1 The Social and Economic Environment

A consideration of the influences on the growth of
literacy among Victorian working class children
must first take account of the social environment
and the economic forces which shaped living
standards and determined the housing conditions in
which the young people lived. For better or worse,
then as now, the home exerted the earliest and most
persistent influence on children. It was there
where they absorbed the attitudes and experiences
of preceding generations which would colour their
outlook and decide their likely reaction to
educational and other influences. There can be
little doubt that parental interest in the
education of children played a vital part in
satisfactory progress at school, and a low level
of literacy could be closely associated with the
indifference or antipathy of parents.

At the beginning of Victoria's reign large
numbers of working class parents were vicious and
depraved, and at a conference in Birmingham in 1861
a speaker referred to them as "slaves of their
lower instincts and passions", who had "no care for
what did not immediately concern their present
needs", and who would not "sacrifice their
convenience or their money to obtain education for

1

their children"(1). Progress in the social and educational system resulted in a gradual improvement in the situation, so that by the late 1880s Charles Booth, the shipowner and statistician, was able to claim that the majority of parents in the lower class did their best for their children however poor that best might have been(2). The attitude of parents was determined by the extent of their own education, for until 1870 only a minority of the working people attended school of any kind, and even after that date many left school before their literacy had been established. The consequence of the limited education which they received, their intellectual outlook was narrow, although to this rule there were of course exceptions who throughout their lives took every opportunity to extend their knowledge.

It is necessary to keep in perspective the reading ability of the working people in early Victorian England. R.K. Webb, an eminent historian, has analysed the results of surveys of reading ability conducted between 1833 and 1848, and he stressed the importance of distinguishing between the ability to read and the desire to read. He criticized the results of surveys which were frequently subject to the bias of politically motivated observers, and to the unwillingness of many people to admit their standard of literacy. Webb pointed out that varying definitions of "reading ability" rendered impossible a reasonable comparison of surveys. Although a working man could be criticized for his inability to master the works of Locke he might still be able to read and enjoy a broadsheet or a working class newspaper. It is also true that the level of literacy varied from one parish to another and was determined by numerous social and economic factors. Webb concluded that complete illiteracy in the 1840s was probably confined to between 20% and 40% of the population, the majority of which belonged to "the very lowest brackets of society".(3)

A rapid acquisition of reading skill by children was likely to be assisted where homes contained books and other reading material as an integral and valued part of daily life. Reading for such children could be seen as an activity which gave their parents enjoyment and which had a purpose. However, in the noisy, overcrowded environment of a

2

slum, or a home in which cottage industry was undertaken it would be difficult for a family to read,
even if it were so inclined, and men who worked for
ten or more hours each day could not reasonably be
expected to read. An observer suggested in 1848
that the family supply of books in ordinary houses
was not only very scanty, but appeared to have
descended as an heirloom for more than one
generation.(4) On the other hand, during the
Lancashire cotton famine in the 1860s, the small
shelves of books in the homes of coliers and
textile workers were noted. After 1870, reading
was usually confined to newspapers, weekly
periodicals, sentimental or sensational novelettes,
and similar items of a trivial character, but even
at the end of the century, the very poor were
unable to afford a half-penny newspaper.

Reading ability was most adequately fostered in
homes where the level of verbal expression among
parents was at its highest; where there was a
feeling for the spoken word as a means of precise
communication; where the vocabulary was rich and
varied; and where children were stimulated by
questions concerning the world beyond their
immediate environment and by explanations which
they could understand. Poorer parents were unable
to provide any of these facilities owing to their
own deficient education. However, those who had
learned to read were still restricted in the time
which they could spend with their children.
Domestic life was almost non-existent when long
hours were spent in the factory, the mine, and on
the land. It was common practice in and after the
1830s for mills in factory areas to be in operation
for fourteen or fifteen hours each day, and during
busy times relays of workers could be occupied for
periods of twenty four hours. The Factories Acts
of 1833, 1844, and 1847 did not restrict the
working day of male workers over eighteen years of
age, although the introduction of the ten hour day
or fifty eight hour week for young people in 1847
rendered it impossible in numerous instances for
adults to continue the work alone. An Act in 1850
provided for the closure of mills on Saturdays at
2.0p.m., but no further concessions were secured
by textile workers until 1874 when the standard
weekly hours were reduced to fifty six and a half.
The numerous Factories Acts between 1850 and 1874
were concerned with the extension of legislation to

3

additional trades rather than with the improvement of conditions for those workers whose employment was already controlled. Engineers at Newcastle-upon-Tyne won a nine hour day in 1871, but in spite of legislation for an eight hour day in 1883, it was not realized until the London gas workers achieved it in 1889. The hours worked by agricultural labourers remained long throughout the century, particularly in the haymaking season and at harvest time, whilst in the winter months the working day was necessarily reduced to seven or eight hours. The benefit of a Saturday half holiday was not generally extended to agriculture, although in the 1890s some workers enjoyed this facility, whilst others were free from 4.0 p.m.

The pattern was for mothers to work, and indeed the first report of the Children's Employment Commission(1842) showed that women were commonly employed underground in the mines of North Lancashire and West Yorkshire, though not in other areas, and the results of such work on the women and their families was graphically described. The Second Commission(1843) exposed the long hours and miserable conditions under which the women worked, sometimes from 5.0 a.m. to 8.30 p.m. Employers who could no longer exploit children owing to the Factories Act of 1833, availed themselves of the poorly paid labour of women, but the latter were included in the same category as young persons in the Act of 1844, that is they worked a twelve hour day or a sixty nine hour week. The Factory and Workshop Act of 1878 stipulated for women a maximum week of fifty six and a half hours in textile factories and sixty hours in non-textile establish-ments.

In the 1850s a wide variety of manual occupations were available to women in London, who assisted in the maintenance of their families by working in small trades.(5)   Charles Booth found that the incomes of families where the father's regular earnings amounted to less than 21/-(£1.05p) per week, the circumstances of 35% of the population, were supplemented by the mother's wages.(6)   In the agricultural areas women abandoned the traditional cottage industry increasingly after 1830 and were hired to hoe turnips or pick stones, and the Poor Law Amendment Act of 1834 resulted in mothers engaging in the field labour under the "gang system" where previously the family had subsisted on the

4

local rates. These women were often absent from their homes from 7.0 a.m. until late in the evening, and at the end of the day were naturally incapable of further exertion. William Booth, the founder of the Salvation Army, remarked that the home was largely destroyed where the mother followed the father into the factory, and where the hours of labour were so long that' they had no time to see their children. He pointed out that "in the countryside, darkness restores the labouring father to his little ones. In the town, gas and the electric light enable the employers to rob the children of the whole of their father's waking hours, and in some cases he takes the mother's also...".(7)

It is true that as there was no security of employment, workers alternated between long hours of labour and periods of idleness, and Charles Booth estimated that the employment of 20% of the population was intermittent,(8) and frequently workers were not completely unemployed but on "short time". The Victorian years were punctuated by periods of unemployment in both industry and agriculture, and in the latter sector was usually determined by the harvest, which was poor during the years 1866-67, 1875-84, and 1891-99. At times of acute poverty, parents were unlikely to be preoccupied with the cultural and educational development of their children, even though they were frequently in their company.

During the Victorian period, the majority of work-ers never ventured beyond their immediate environ-ment, although some Londoners enjoyed annual charity and club excursions to Epping, Hampton Court, and even to the seaside. Seebohm Rowntree found that at York many skilled workers had a few days holiday in Scarborough, whilst others benefited from cheap railway excursions,(9) and H.D. Traill commented that a country holiday was considered a necessity by all classes except the very poor.(10) Therefore,in the closing decades of the 19th century, there was evidence of an increased availability of leisure, which could have influenced the growth of literacy through the relationships of parents with their children.

The size of Victorian families must be seen as a factor in educational progress. It is recognized

that children with three or more siblings are
likely to be at a disadvantage when compared with
their peers in smaller families, a contrast which
has been most evident in the children of manual
workers. In 1860, families of four or more children
constituted almost three quarters of the population,
and families of agricultural workers, miners, and
unskilled labourers were larger than the average.
However, there was a tendency to marry later, so
that whilst the proportion of those who married
between the ages of twenty and twenty four reached
a peak of about 28% between 1846 and 1851, it
declined to 19% between 1886 and 1891. From the
institution of the registration of births and
deaths in 1837, the birth rate always exceeded the
death rate, but after 1880 the rate of increase
began to decline.(11) It was suggested that this
was owing to a continuous decrease in the marriage
rate after 1850,(12) but this is an erroneous
conclusion. The marriage rate fluctuated slightly
from 1850, and increased somewhat in the 1870s, but
the proportion of people who married at an age when
they could normally have children was fairly stable
at all times. The fall in the birth rate has been
closely related to the trial of Charles Bradlaugh
and Annie Besant during 1877-78, and the widespread
discussion of contraception which arose from it;
the withdrawal of children from employment in and
after 1870; and the period of economic depression
which existed during the last three decades of the
century. The combined effects of the two latter
factors served to render large families a luxury
which the working people could not afford, Other
factors which are claimed to have assisted in the
decline of the birth rate include higher standards
of parental care, the growing interest in science
and social reform, and the gradually improved
status of women in society.(13) It was not
however until some time later that the contraceptive
habits began to be adopted by the working people,
and during the 1890s the poor economic state of
almost 30% of the population was partly attribut-
able to large families.(14)

There could be little doubt that the general
progress of children who were not living with both
their natural parents was likely to be less
satisfactory than that of children who lived with
both parents. Premature widowhood was widespread

in the 1830s, and not surprisingly remarriage
amongst women with children was rare. The hazards
of factory labour shortened the duration of life
to the extent that in a sample of 100 children,
probably thirty fathers would be deceased,(15) and
a vast amount of individual suffering and family
deprivation resulted. Successive industrial
legislation ensured the improvement in working
conditions, but in the 1870s the average length of
life of factory workers was thirty eight to forty
years, that of the miner only thirty, as compared
with the professional man's fifty years.(16) The
mortality rate of almost all occupations declined
during the 1890s, with the exception of the hosiery
and lace industry, and in copper and tin mining,
but even at the turn of the century, occupational
diseases caused many thousands of deaths each year.
In addition, the migration of workers to large
urban areas which were not equipped to absorb them
resulted in a rise in the death rate during the
forty years prior to 1850, which did not begin to
fall decisively until after 1870 when a programme
of building and sanitary development was initiated.
The mortality of inhabitants in rural districts was
approximately 23% lower than that of urban districts
in 1902.(17)

The physical condition of parents had a direct
influence on their attitude to the well-being of
their children. The consequences to health of
unsatisfactory housing and sanitation are referred
to later in the present chapter, but of equal or
even greater importance was the danger in Victorian
times to health inherent in numerous employments
in which the working people were engaged. In the
course of their labours, miners and factory workers
suffered complaints caused by high temperatures and
the presence of impurities in the atmosphere, which
combined to undermine their health and vitality.
Numerous industries were subject to metal and other
poisoning, but others were injurious to health
through the absence of adequate sanitation and
ventilation. As early as 1842, Edwin Chadwick, the
sociologist and journalist, pointed out the
distinction which must be drawn between industries
subject to inherent occupational diseases and those
in which causes of ill-health were accidental and
not essential to the employment.(18) Sanitary
legislation was not applied to factories until 1864,
when certain trades, for example match-makers and

7

potters, were protected; and again in 1867, when
the law was extended. Textile factories were not
embraced by this legislation however until 1878.
Although many employers throughout the Victorian
period realized that lighting, sanitation, and
ventilation could be economically profitable to
them as they were beneficial to employees; the
improvements in industrial hygiene which took place
during the last four decades of the century could
not influence immediately the health of an
enfeebled working population. In addition, physical
deterioration was caused not only by factory
employment but by the intemperate habits of
parents, which were transmitted in poor health to
succeeding generations.

In order to estimate the ability of the working
people to educate their children, it is necessary
to examine their standard of living. A low level of
real wages in relation to prices was an unfavourable
influence on the growth of literacy. A poor socio-
economic status was detrimental to nutrition,
living conditions, and expenditure on such items as
school fees, books and other reading material for
educational and recreational purposes.

<u>1837-1850</u> There is no consensus of opinion as to
whether real wages improved in the first half of
the 19th century, owing to the fact that insufficient is known about retail prices. Certainly, the
years 1836 to 1843 were among the worst in an
economic sense through which this country has ever
passed, and whilst prices rose, wages remained
low. The decade 1840 to 1850 showed a decrease in
prices of approximately 30%, mainly after 1847, and
although earnings fell slightly between 1825 and
1845, it was not sufficient to outweigh the real
gain. With the exception of the rapidly declining
condition of handloom weavers, other workers in
domestic industries, and possibly agricultural
labourers, the working people benefited from a slow
but persistent increase in the purchasing power of
their incomes. However, the Census of 1831 showed
that 28% of the families of Great Britain were
employed in agriculture; in 1851 the proportion was
similar, and the largest single group of workers
still laboured on the land.(19) It is impossible
to generalize on the standard of agricultural
labourers, which varied greatly between counties

where industry had developed to compete for their services, and those where no competition existed.

1850-1875 A general rise of 33% in real wages took place between 1850 and 1875, for skilled workers in full employment, but little is known of the fortunes of the unskilled. Trades in which earnings were poor in 1850, gained more than those in which there was already a fair standard of living. In agriculture, real wages were in 1874 approximately 50% above the level of 1850, but workers were, as now, paid much less than those in industry. Between 1850 and 1870, the numbers of agricultural labourers decreased by almost 20%, but in spite of this, more workers were still employed in agriculture than in any other single industry.(20)

1875-1901 Prices rose sharply between 1872 and 1873, but from the latter date their fall was much greater than that of wages until 1896. Therefore the standard of living of the majority of workers continued to improve. After 1896, retail prices rose and generally neutralized the wage rises of the later 1890s, but real wages in 1900 were in fact approximately 50% higher than in 1850. The decline of agriculture in and after the 1870s resulted in an accelerated movement to the towns. However, by 1901 the population of urban districts in England and Wales was still only 62% of the total, but the largest single groups were in transport and the metal industry rather than in agriculture.(21)

Whilst the condition of the working class improved appreciably throughout the Victorian period, Charles Booth in 1891 and Seebohm Rowntree in 1901 showed that the progress was relative. Booth defined the poor as those whose means were barely sufficient to maintain an independent standard of life, and who earned 18/-(90p) to 21/-(£1.05p) per week. He divided the working people into six groups, and showed that the income of families in four of them, that is 35% of the total, was absorbed by necessary expenditure, and that clothes could be purchased only by evading the payment of rent or by curtailing the supply of food.(22) Booth's investigations were made in East London in the years 1886 to 1888. The conditions which Rowntree discovered in York in 1899 were not exceptional and were fairly representative of many provincial towns. Rowntree divided the working population in his survey into four groups, two of

which were usually above the poverty line. He
calculated that almost 30% of the population of
York was living in poverty, and families in that
condition "must never purchase a half penny newspaper or spend a penny to buy a ticket for a
popular concert...never contribute anything to
their church or chapel, or give any help to a
neighbour which costs them money...". Such
families were unable to save, the children
received no pocket money, and the wage earners
must never be absent from work for a single day.(23)

The standard of living, precarious as it was, was
subject to unemployment due to industrial depression and redundancy in the towns; to the vagaries
of the weather and an inability after 1870 to
compete with foreign agriculture in country
districts; and to strikes. Reference has been made
to the hazards of industrial accidents and
diseases, for which there was little compensation,
and then only through insurance schemes until the
passing of the Employers' Liability Act of 1880.
The benefits of this and the Workmen's Compensation
Act of 1897 were not extended to agricultural
labourers until 1907.

Uneconomical methods of housekeeping by women
ignorant of any form of domestic economy
contributed to their poverty, as did the high
prices which were charged by shopkeepers to
customers who relied on them for credit in times
of distress. Throughout the period the financial
problems of the working people were alleviated to
a limited extent by friendly societies, which
developed in the 1830s and 1840s; working men's
clubs, in and after the 1850s; and co-operative
societies, the activities of which were legalized
in 1852. Trade unions were increasingly beneficial
to skilled workers. It would be wrong to assume
that all working people were unable to save some
of their income, although large sections were
unable to do so. At the time of the cotton famine
of the 1860s it was apparent that some had
accumulated small sums of money which they had
invested in savings banks, but these resources were
quickly dispersed during the period of
unemployment.(24)

There was clearly an association between various
aspects of children's development and housing
conditions. The general progress of children at

school was adversely affected by poor housing, but other factors must of course be taken into consideration, such as the permanence or otherwise of overcrowding and the size and composition of a household. It is important to recognize that, whilst it cannot be determined what proportion of the population lived under housing conditions which were conducive to bad health at the outset of Victoria's reign, the potential dangers can be computed. In the first decade the problem was aggravated by the ever increasing movement of population into towns unable to accommodate it, particularly during the Irish hunger of 1845-46. Similar and frequently more severe overcrowding was evident in the cottages of rural areas. Contemporary conditions have been well documented by such observers as Chadwick, Friedrich Engels, Henry Mayhew, and Hippolyte Taine, and there is no need to reiterate their findings at this point.

In all large towns the average number of persons living in a house declined from 5.32 in 1891 to 5.20 in 1901, but these averages were not significantly different from 1841 when the overcrowding figure was 5.44.(25) The Registrar General defined overcrowding as existing where the average number of persons per room was more than two. In 1891 therefore, the percentage of overcrowding in Gateshead was 40, in Newcastle-upon-Tyne 35, in Bradford 20, in Birmingham 14, in Liverpool 10, and in Manchester 8.(26) At no time did housing development equate with the increase in population.

In certain circumstances working class houses were available for tenancy, and at the time of commercial distress in 1841 it was claimed that in Stockport one house in five was empty, because the factory operatives were unable to pay their rent.(27) This situation was also observed at Bolton, Preston, and other towns at that time. In the 1880s there were sufficient houses in London for all who could pay for them, especially in suburbs such as Edmonton, Enfield, and Tottenham, where a large proportion of the houses were unoccupied.(28) The percentage of overcrowding in 1891 was low at Nottingham(3%), Derby(2.75%), and Leicester(2.25%).(29) In country districts there was a lack of accommodation in some villages, whilst increasingly in others there was a superfluity of cottages owing to the migration of agricultural labourers to the towns.

Chadwick's report in 1842 was devoted partly to an examination of the correlation between insanitation, defective drainage, inadequate water supply, and overcrowding on the one hand, and disease and poor health on the other. This represented an important development in social ideas, but from this time the absence of sanitation and the other requisites of health were the subject of detailed comments in the reports of observers throughout the 19th century, from those of Chadwick and the Buccleuch Commission on The State of Large Towns (1844), to Charles Booth. However, the improvements which were recommended by Chadwick and the Buccleuch Commission required resources which were not then available and techniques which were not known. The bacteriological cause of disease was not established until after 1870.

There were vital personal reasons why large numbers of working class parents remained in the unhygienic conditions which existed. Many were compelled to do so owing to poverty and could not afford to pay the rents which were demanded for superior accommodation, and as a palliative to their distress they frequently drank to excess. In numerous instances, slum clearance was not accompanied by a rebuilding programme and residents were driven into even more unsatisfactory environments. It was necessary too for workmen to live in reasonably close proximity to their occupations, particularly dockers and market porters. Agricultural labourers had very little choice of accommodation until the period of depression in and after the 1870s.

Legislation took the form of local government, housing and sanitary reforms. Progress was slow and by 1848 only twenty nine boroughs had made use of their powers acquired in the Municipal Corporations Act of 1835. It was not until 1894 that a system of parish councils was established in rural areas to replace the boards of guardians and other local bodies as sanitary authorities. Numerous local building acts were passed between 1825 and 1850, but their effectiveness was minimal. Acts between 1850 and 1880 strengthened the powers of local authorities regarding separate houses, whilst others between 1870 and 1900 were concerned with the demolition and reconstruction of whole areas. But these Acts were adopted slowly by the local authorities, and there was no widespread public intervention in housing until after the Housing of the Working Classes Act of 1890. The establishment of the office of Registrar General in 1837 resulted in the provision of statistical information relating to public health, and Chadwick's report pointed out the need for an administrative framework, but the Public Health Act of 1848 was only permissive. Progress was made in 1866 with the mandatory requirement that local authorities must appoint sanitary inspectors; in 1871 with the establishment of the Local Government Board which was not always helpful to local bodies in the realization of their programmes; in 1872 with the extension of sanitary law to rural areas; and in 1875 with the Public Health Act. The 1848 Act did not make provision for London and the situation in this respect was not rectified until 1891.

Although progress was slow it is also true however that even where efficient improvements were made, inhabitants, owing to ignorance, were frequently careless of their own health, throwing refuse into their gardens or yards, which formed "a putrescent heap around which the children play".(30) It was important to awaken in the poor a sense of self respect, self-restraint, and a desire for decency and order.

In addition to municipal enterprise the improvement of housing conditions was assisted to a small extent by individuals and organizations both charitable and commercial. Manufacturers erected accommodation for their employees, such as the model villages of Crossley & Ackroyd at Halifax in the 1860s. In London the Metropolitan Sanitary Society and the Labourer's Friend Society, and other bodies supported by voluntary subscriptions, improved dwellings as, on a commercial basis did the Metropolitan Association for the Improvement of the Dwellings of the Labouring Classes in the 1850s. Octavia Hill was engaged for many years in the improvement of houses for the Ecclesiastical Commissioners, and the Guinness and Peabody Trusts erected model tenements between 1870 and the end of the century. In country districts there was no effective local government control of housing and sanitation until after 1894, but many landlords throughout the 19th century provided well constructed cottages for labourers employed on their estates. Some of the more outstanding examples in the early part of the reign belonged to the Earls of Leicester and Stradbroke at Holkham and Henham, and Gregory Gregory at Harlaxton. In the 1880s, model cottages were in existence on the estates of the Queen at Sandringham, the Russell's at Woburn, and the Percy's at Alnwick.

In 1837 there was no sanitary legislation and fever was endemic in neighbourhoods where poverty and unsatisfactory living conditions existed. Chadwick pointed out that however defective the factories were, all were drier and more equably warm than the majority of homes.(31) In the 1830s there was a resurgance of smallpox, and even in 1871 there was a serious epidemic; cholera, the result of inadequate water supplies,first appeared in 1831, and returned in 1848, 1854, and 1867; there were outbreaks of typhus in 1837 and 1846, which was aggravated by social distress and living conditions. Most virulent of all was tuberculosis, a result of undernourishment and poor ventilation. Diphtheria commenced as a world epidemic in 1858 and persisted as a fatal endemic disease until the late 19th century, when it was increasingly combated by antitoxins. Many claimed to trace disease in the 1840s to Irish immigrants, and indeed, typhus was at its most virulent in times of famine. Doctors on the other hand recognized the causes as emanating from poverty and unsanitary conditions. Even in 1850 however, qualified doctors were few, and the majority of inhabitants of this country never benefited from medical treatment. Vaccination only became free in England in 1840, was made compulsory for all infants in 1853, but was not widely adopted until after 1865. The threat to health of cholera, scarlet fever, smallpox, tuberculosis, and typhus diminished rapidly during and after the decade 1866-1875 owing to improved sanitation and more accessible medical facilities.

It is reasonable to suggest that the personalities of parents, particularly mothers, could greatly influence the problems of unsatisfactory living conditions. Damp and dirt were features of large numbers of Victorian working class homes, and the furnishings were pathetically inadequate, but it seemed probable that if people were better housed they would be less likely to spend their earnings on beer, and would be encouraged to spend more time at home. They would in addition be more likely to become better parents to their children. There can be no doubt that in numerous instances these were likely results of improved environments. However, even in the poorest areas, some of the homes were kept clean and tidy and their inhabitants lived in comparative comfort and contentment, at least in periods when their endeavours were not frustrated by unemployment.

It is unlikely that the habit of reading was widespread in overcrowded homes devoid of all comfort, even where a basic literacy had been attained. When more enlightened parents ensured to the best of their ability a comfortable environment, paralleled by the acquisition of reading ability, books were likely to have a place in the home. However, for most of the Victorian period the opportunities for leisure were restricted and reading in the home was inevitably limited to Sunday and weekday evenings. In the winter activity of this kind was directly influenced by the artificial lighting which was available, and where there was little or no natural light, the influence was perennial.The presence or absence of lighting in the home was a very important factor in social history, but there is very little precise information available regarding its availability to the working people. References to the use of candles, fires, rushes, and, very occasionally, oil lamps, are made in some of the novels of Charles Dickens, George Eliot, Elizabeth Gaskell, and other writers. Similar evidence is given in the autobiographical reminiscences of such writers as Richard Church in Over the Bridge(Heinemann, 1955), A.L. Rowse in A Cornish Childhood(Cape, 1942), and Emlyn Williams in George: an early autobiography(Hamish Hamilton, 1961). These writers bear testimony to the use of gas lighting in the working class homes of late Victorian England. In the first decade of the reign, the light most easily afforded by the poor was the rush dipped in tallow, which gave a reasonably clear light. Candles were expensive and their price tended to rise, were unsatisfactory in that they smoked or guttered, and the position of the light altered as they became smaller. Rush-

lights and short candles cost $\frac{1}{2}$d., coal was
expensive, and, in most country districts, not
easily accessible. In London however, coal could
be purchased from mudlarks for as little as 1d.
for 14lbs., or more usually, for 2d.(32)

However, the manufacture of candles from paraffin
wax in the 1860s resulted in their becoming cheaper
and improved, whilst paraffin oil made the use of
lamps more extensive in both urban and rural areas.
Between 1805 and 1865, gas lighting spread rapidly,
not only into streets but also into houses. Gas
was in fact cheaper than all other forms of lighting in the 1860s, but in areas where the population
was scattered the cost of distribution was
prohibitive. The gas was dirty and had an
unpleasant smell, but in the 1890s, technical
progress ensured improvement. The consolidation of
gas lighting in the homes of the poor was effected
after 1892, when the penny slot meter was introduced
In addition, the last decade of the century
witnessed not only the introduction of the incan-
descent gas mantle, but also the substitution of
water gas on an increasing scale, for coal gas.
The former cost less to produce and sell, and
burned with greater heat than the latter. Unfortunately, the working people often used their gas
supply unwisely, burning more than was necessary,
and adjusting the fitting so that either
insufficient illumination or a smoky flame was
produced. Electric lighting was not a feature of
working class domestic life during the Victorian
period, although in view of its competitive
potential, the gas companies endeavoured to lower
their prices and improve their service.

It is not possible to estimate the number of
those working class children in Victorian England
whose educational development was adversely
influenced by social and economic factors. For the
majority however, it is reasonable to suggest that
the potential influence of their environment was
negative. Most of the social and economic factors
which were to exercise a beneficial influence on
the growth of literacy were absent before 1870,
and none of them achieved their full fruition in
the 19th century.

REFERENCES

1   Ratcliff, C., _Ragged schools in relation to government grants for education_, p.22.
2   Booth, C.(ed.), _Labour and life of the people_, Vol.2, p.495.
3   Webb, R.K. Working class readers in early Victorian England, _English Historical Review_, 65(1950), pp.333-51.
4   Ritchie, L., Article literature, _Chambers's Edinburgh Journal_, 9(1848), p.193.
5   Anonymous, Employments of women, _Chambers's Edinburgh Journal_, 20(1853), p.156.
6   Booth, C.(ed.), op. cit., Vol.1, p.50.
7   Booth, W., _In darkest England_, p.64.
8   Booth, C.(ed.), op. cit., Vol.1, pp.43-4.
9   Rowntree, B.S., _Poverty_, p.76.
10 Traill, H.D.(ed.), _Social England_,Vol.6, p.642.
11 Registrar General, _Annual report_, 1898, p.lxi; Royal Commission on Population, _Report_(1949), pp.26, 27, 72.
12 Porter, G.R., _Progress of the nation_, pp.13-14.
13 The influences of feminism as a causal factor has been refuted by J.A. and O. Banks in _Feminism and family planning in Victorian England_, (Liverpool University Press, 1964).
14 Rowntree, B.S., op. cit., pp.119-45.
15 Anonymous, The factory system, _Quarterly Review_, 57(1836), p.437.
16 Escott, T.H.S., _England_, Vol.1, p.275.
17 Porter, G.R., op. cit., p.10.
18 Chadwick, E., _Report on the sanitary condition of the labouring population in Great Britain_, p.255.
19 Census of Great Britain(1851), _Population tables_(1852), Vol.1, pp.lxix-lxx, xcix.
20 Census of England and Wales(1871), _General report_(1873), pp.iv, 111.
21 Census of England and Wales(1901), _Preliminary report_(1901), p.20; _General report_(1904),p.82.
22 Booth, C.(ed.), op. cit., Vol.1, pp.33, 135-8.
23 Rowntree, B.S., op. cit., pp.vi, 31-73, 118, 133-4.
24 Watts, J., _The facts of the cotton famine_,p.84; Waugh, E., _Home life of the Lancashire factory folk_, p.94.
25 Porter, G.R., op. cit., pp.91-2.
26 Rowntree, B.S., op. cit., pp.169-71.
27 Hutchins, B.L. and Harrison, A., _A history of factory legislation_, 3rd ed., p.64.

28   International Health Exhibition, _Literature_,
         Vol.2, p.26.
29   Rowntree, B.S., op. cit., p.171.
30   International Health Exhibition, op. cit.,
         Vol.1, p.25; Vol.2, p.6.
31   Chadwick, E., op. cit., p.223.
32   Mayhew, H., _London labour and the London poor_,
         Vol.1, p.428; Vol.2, p.173.

2 School Provision and Attendance

For hundreds of years schools had been established for the purpose of instructing poor children, but even in the 19th century their provision was isolated. Children were taught to read in Sunday schools but these proved inadequate to meet the demand for literacy, and it was considered necessary to organize a national system of day schools.

Prior to 1870 the education of the poor in the 19th century was undertaken principally by religious organizations,(1) which included the National Society(1811), the Wesleyan Education Committee(1840), the Congregational Board of Education(1843), and the Catholic Poor School Committee(1847). The National Society together with the non-sectarian British and Foreign School Society(1808), were the most influential, and in 1846 the schools of the former contained 912,000 pupils, whilst those of the latter contained almost 200,000.(2) National schools did not only include children who belonged to the Anglican church, although this has been frequently disputed. In 1867 there were 1,355 parishes in England and Wales in which schools had been established by the Church of England, and most of the facilities were quite inadequate for the

population involved. Although school boards were s
up after 1870 in an attempt to ensure that a
national system of education was available, a
considerable expansion also took place in the
provision of voluntary schools. In 1900, voluntary
schools still made provision for almost 300,000
more children than did the board schools.(3)

Dames' schools were widespread in both urban and
rural areas, but were frequently little more than
nurseries in which young children were minded whil
their parents were at work. They were mainly quite
unsuitable for educational purposes although
exceptions were to be found. Private schools were
popular with many parents who were not in a state
of poverty, because they considered that their
children would be less exposed to infectious
diseases, rough behaviour, and bad language. Even
after 1870 there were still a much decreased
number of private and dames' schools in existence,
and whilst Inspectors were powerless to close them
many local authorities refused to do so. An
Inspector at Taunton in 1880 commented on local
authorities who would not "undertake the unpopular-
ity of so directly closing the only means that some
worthy illiterate woman has of earning her
livelihood".(4)

Factory owners frequently opened schools in their
mills from 1833 in order to conform to the terms of
the Factories Act of that year. All children aged
between nine and thirteen who were employed in
textile factories must provide their employers with
certificates confirming that they had attended
school for minimum of two hours on each of the six
days of the preceding week. In the absence of
schools in the district, owners made their own
provision, but the form which the curriculum was
to take was not defined, and frequently children
received no instruction of any value. Employers
tended to engage as teachers their female dependents
or workmen who were incapacitated, or the
responsibility was delegated to employees who
combined the office of teacher with their existing
occupation. Many of these "teachers" were
unsuitable and often illiterate, and although from
1833 Inspectors were empowered to dismiss those who
were unsatisfactory, there were insufficient
Inspectors initially to exercise a significant
influence. Only 20% of the 427 factory schools in

the North of England in 1851 were considered to be
efficient,(5) and in 1861 Nassau Senior, the
political economist, drew attention to the

> repeated representations...made without
> effect to the occupiers of extensive
> works, as to the inefficient state and
> condition of the schools under their
> immediate control.   (6)

Although the Poor Law Amendment Act of 1834
ensured that children in workhouses should receive
three hours instruction each day, no facilities
were available to large numbers of children whose
parents were unable or unwilling to dress them
suitably or provide them with regular meals.
Managers of National schools were usually adamant
that pupils should be tidily dressed and punctual
in their attendance , and the latter requirement
was not easily satisfied by children who were fed
irregularly. Whilst it is true that schools for
poorer children existed in the 1830s, their number
increased substantially after the Ragged School
Union was founded in 1844, and in 1861 those in
London alone contained more than 20,000 children.
These children are said to have comprised three
broad groups: those whose parents were dissipated,
receiving outdoor relief, or could afford to pay
for education, and would have sent their children
to school had establishments of this kind not
existed.(7) In the ragged schools, the care of
clothing and punctuality were not insisted upon,
and it was questionable whether the children
derived any significant educational benefit in the
majority of instances. Many of the schools were
situated in unsuitable premises, and a particularly
notorious example at Bermondsey, was held in a
railway tunnel. Most of the ragged schools were
closed after 1870.

Evening schools were available to serve the needs
of children who were at work during the day. They
were established in the 1830s, there being some in
Liverpool in 1836.(8) Large numbers were opened
in the 1840s which were generally attended by
young people from twelve years of age. The pupils
usually received instruction in the three Rs
between the hours of 7 or 8 p.m. and 9 or 10 p.m.,
from the master of the local National school.
Evening schools were popular in industrial areas,
such as the Potteries and Liverpool, but not in
agricultural districts where the distances to be

21

travelled were too great, nor in mining
communities were the sessions were incompatible
with the shift work of colliery labour. These
schools played an important part in elementary
education until the 1880s when the extension of
the Education Acts rendered them superfluous. The
Cross Commission recommended in 1888 that evening
schools should be concerned with further education
rather than with elementary instruction,(9) and
this was implemented in the Evening Continuation
Code of 1893.

The voluntary system of education was dependent
on private benevolence for its continuance, and
frequently the local clergy were entirely
responsible for whatever facilities were available
Farmers and country gentlemen in rural areas were
not generous in their contributions, although
there were notable exceptions. There were instance
where the local squirearchy was very generous in
its support of elementary schools, but in other
cases educational facilities would have been non-
existent had not the clergy subscribed money from
their stipends, and even at the end of the century
the situation in some schools was precarious.

Throughout the reign of Victoria the inherent
financial weakness of the voluntary system was
overcome in part by government grants which had
commenced in 1833, when £20,000 was allocated to
the building of schools by the National and
British societies. After 1846, the other voluntary
bodies became eligible for assistance on conformin
to the Management Clauses of that year. However, a
all times the managers of many schools were unable
to improve their facilities to an extent which
would enable them to qualify for grants, and
although the number of inspected schools in 1858
was 6,897, the uninspected establishments totalled
15,952.(10) In 1869 only 50% of the schools were
under inspection. The funds at the disposal of the
Committee of Council were limited, and in 1850
Joseph Kay, the economist, estimated that the
grant of £125,000, which was distributed throughout England, Scotland, and Wales, was not sufficie
for the provision of a satisfactory standard of
education in the county of Cheshire.(11) The
distribution of grants was made, subject to
satisfactory reports from Inspectors, and
government expenditure increased steadily until
1862, when the Revised Code stipulated that grants

22

must be awarded on the basis of satisfactory examination results rather than in the existing form of stipends for pupil-teachers, augmented salaries for certificated teachers, and <u>per capita</u> grants for pupils. The influence on education of the Revised Code will be discussed in Chapter 5, but it is relevant to state that from a financial point of view, the variable character of the new grant undermined the stability of schools, even though the total grant increased substantially after 1870. In 1886 the government contributed approximately 42% of the income of elementary schools, but as a result of the Code of 1890 a generous fixed grant was introduced in addition to the larger variable allowance, the former being awarded according to the general standard of each school and the quality of the work which was produced. Further progress was effected in 1900 when the fixed and variable payments were amalgamated into a single grant. Until 1857, ragged schools did not receive grants of any kind from the government because they did not normally include certificated teachers or pupil-teachers, and they did not attain a state which could be regarded as satisfactory to Inspectors. In 1857 however a limited sum was allocated to ragged industrial schools, but in spite of protests, it was not extended to non-industrial establishments. The government grant to education in 1861 was £1,200,000, of which ragged schools received the niggardly sum of about £5,000.(12)

Although the religious organizations were eager to provide educational facilities for working class children, most of them were strongly opposed to the government becoming involved in what they regarded as their monopoly, and this factor proved retrogressive to the extension of literacy in England. In the Victorian period, the security of Lord Melbourne's administration was threatened when an attempt was made to institute a secular training college for teachers in 1839, the educational clauses of the Factory Bill of 1843 were defeated, as were successive educational Bills promoted by private members between 1850 and 1869. John Morley, the Liberal statesman and man of letters, accused the Anglican Church of traditional obstruction to the growth of English liberties;(13) whilst Archdeacon Manning and other high Anglicans denied that the secular power had any duty other

23

than financial in education.(14) It is probable that the majority of the clergy were prepared to co-operate with the government in improving the situation which existed prior to 1870, and certainly the Wesleyans were favourable to this as early as 1846. The various voluntary bodies accepted grants as they became available, with the exception of the Congregationalists. Some politicians believed that the control of education should be transferred completely to the government, but in 1870, W.E. Forster, the Vice President of the Council, insisted on the principle of dual control, a policy which was reaffirmed in the report of the Cross Commission in 1888.(15) The promoters of voluntary schools were allowed six months in which to remedy defects in their provision, and if they wished, their schools could be transferred to the new school boards. In practice, the subscriptions to voluntary schools increased substantially, so that between 1870 and 1880 it was possible to add more than 1 million places to existing facilities.

Whilst elementary education was made available to all classes of society after 1870, there was very little progress in the provision for working class children who wished to undertake a course in secondary education. The Taunton Commission reported in 1868 that there was an urgent need for good schools which would cater for children aged fourteen or fifteen, and recommended that such schools should either be attached to elementary schools which were under inspection, or that they should constitute a separate group. It should have been possible for promising boys in elementary schools to be promoted without the requirement from parents of an extra payment.(16) The Bryce Commission on Secondary Education in its report in 1895, advocated the formation of a strong, progressive central authority to supervise the activities of local bodies taking part in secondary education,(17) and in 1899, provision was made for the amalgamation of the three principal authorities entrusted with the oversight of elementary, secondary, and technical education. A Board of Education for this purpose was formally established in 1900.

During the 1890s, some school boards and voluntary

bodies in England introduced an extra Standard, whilst others established higher grade elementary schools, which were in fact secondary in character, in order to cater for the increased number of children who were remaining at school for a longer period. In 1894, seventeen secondary schools had been founded or were being founded by county councils in collaboration with the Charity Commissioners, governing bodies of endowed schools, or school boards. Forty two of the forty eight counties were spending part of their funds on scholarships, the majority of which were for children from elementary schools, but county boroughs had undertaken very little work of this kind. The need for a larger supply of scholarships was emphasized by the Bryce Commission for the transfer of pupils in higher grade schools to grammar schools.(18) However inadequate the provision, in the 1890s it was possible for some working class children to remain at day school engaged in secondary studies until they were eighteen, and all could continue their education at evening classes unless geographical factors prevented them from doing so.

The opportunity for employment was an obstacle to children in Victorian England attending school. Until the reports of the Children's Employment Commission in 1842 and 1843 however, there was no precise information available as to the early age at which children commenced work, the long hours they worked, the nature of their employment, and the harmful effects of this on their health. In 1861 the children of almost 90% of the population were not at school, and a majority were estimated to be in employment.(19) Throughout the period restrictions were increasingly placed on the employment of children by legislation. As has been seen, the Factories Act of 1833 required that all children aged from nine to thirteen who worked in textile mills must attend school for at least two hours each day. Unfortunately schools were not always available, many employers evaded the spirit of the law whenever possible, and there were insufficient Inspectors to ensure that the legislation was effective. The 1844 Act obliged children to spend either three whole days or six half days in school, and in this way "half-time" education was commenced, which was particularly prevalent in Lancashire throughout the Victorian period. The Factory Acts Extension Act of 1864 standardized education provision and was extended to almost all branches of manual labour in 1867 with the exception of the large agricultural group. Children in rural areas were not protected at all until the Agricultural Gangs Act of 1867 which excluded from employment all aged seven and younger, and the Agricultural Children Act of 1873, which raised the minimum age to ten. Although the factory law contained educational clauses, its purpose was to restrict employment, and the insistence on school attendance was solely a means of ensuring its effectiveness. Unfortunately the factory law was not easily operable in rural areas, nor were the means of inspection adequate in the industrial areas, particularly in the small workshops which were protected in 1867.

There was considerable confusion as to the clauses of the Factories Acts in relation to the Education Acts after 1870. The Elementary Education Act of 1876 stated that children under ten could not be employed under any circumstances, and those aged ten to thirteen could, only if they attained a prescribed standard of education or attendance. In contradiction to this, the Factory and Workshop Act of 1878 continued to permit half-time employment in factories without the requirement of an educational qualification. However, the situation was regulated in the Education Act of 1880, when the compulsory framing of byelaws by local authorities was regarded as repealing the relevant clauses in the existing factory law. From 1880 no child could be absent from school under any circumstances without a certificate of educational attainment. The apparent conflict in legislation was resolved in the factory and education laws of 1891 and 1893, when the former raised the minimum age for the employment of children in factories to eleven, and the latter raised the school leaving age to the same level. However, a major defect in the law as regards "half-time" education was the fact that children only attended school when they were actually employed, but tended to be absent in periods of unemployment. Also, if they passed the half-time Standard at nine or ten, their attendance was usually irregular until they left school at eleven, or from 1899, at twelve.

The authority of the educational byelaws as an overruling factor was the subject of legal disputes for the last three decades of Victoria's reign. The phraseology of the Education Acts was vague and as such could not be adequately used as evidence in a court of law. In 1901 it was clear that new legislation was essential

It is useful to evaluate the influence of legislation after 1870 on school attendance. In 1870, it was estimated that about 1,500,000 children were on the registers of inspected schools, but an equal number either did not attend school at all, or attended establishments which were unsuitable for educational purposes. As a result of the Education Act of 1870, in 1873 there were 2,218,598 children on the registers of aided schools, that is approximately 74% of those who should have been enrolled. The average annual percentage increase in the years 1874 to 1877 was 9.14, but in each of these years there was a steady decline in the rate of increase from 12.25% to 7.17%.

Between the Education Acts of 1876 and 1880 the average annual percentage increase fell to 7.29%, but an annual increase in 1878 of 10.8% was remarkable indeed. The Act of 1880 does not appear to have significantly influenced the annual rate of increase, which fell from 6.11% in 1879 to 1.73% in 1885. This was followed by a slight revival in 1886 and 1887 after which the decline continued from an increase of 1.13% in 1888 to 0.43% in 1891. Following the abolition of fees, the annual rate of increase rose to 3.78% in 1892, after which the fall was almost continuous until 1900. It is clear then that the greatest influence on school attendance was felt during the 1870s, before the framing of byelaws was made obligatory. No further dramatic influence can be attributed to either the Act of 1880 or those of 1893 and 1899. However, the abolition of fees in 1891 resulted in an immediate stimulus, which as an annual increase had not been achieved since 1881. The average annual percentage increase from 1881 to 1891 was approximately 2%, as compared with 8.36% from 1874 to 1880, and 1.84% from 1892 to 1900. The influence of the school leaving laws on the rate of increase cannot be dismissed however, for it is possible that without them it would have fallen more rapidly, especially as the birthrate declined after 1877. In 1900 there were 5,705,675 children on the registers of aided schools, whereas on the basis of 16.66% of the population being of school age, there ought to have been slightly more than 6,000,000 enrolled. Therefore educational legislation had failed to account for about 13% of the children of school age.

The average daily attendance of children in aided schools after 1870 was however far lower than the numbers who were enrolled:

	Children on the Registers	Children in Average Daily Attendance
1873	2,218,598(73.95%)	1,482,480(49.42%)
1880	3,895,824(77.92%)	2,750,916(55.02%)
1885	4,412,148(80.22%)	3,371,325(61.1%)
1890	4,804,149(81.61%)	3,717,919(63.2%)
1895	5,299,469(87.12%)	4,325,030(71.13%)
1900	5,705,675(87.78%	4,687,646(72.12%) (20)

The number of children on the registers did not reach 80% until 1885, and the average daily attendance did not rise above 70% until the mid-1890s.

In 1870 the average length of school life was 2.55 years; in 1880, 5.19 years; in 1890, 6.13 years; and in 1897, 7.05 years. Thus from 1870 to 1897, the length of school life was almost trebled.(21) Inspectors in 1870 claimed that children who attended school for less than four years would not normally enjoy any permanent benefit from their educational experience. In terms of the Act of 1876, the necessary length of time to be spent at school was five years; the Act of 1893, six years; and the Act of 1899, seven years. The average length of school life did not increase sufficiently therefore to be beneficial to children until 1880.

In the immediate years after 1870, the deficiencies in educational provision were ascertained and the organization created for their removal. It was necessary for sufficient schools and competent teachers to be made available before any salutory improvement in attendance could be realized. The educational structure was strengthened in 1872 when 2,817 parishes were compulsorily amalgamated into 989 united districts; in 1876 when provision was made for the appointment of school attendance committees in every borough and

parish for which a school board had not been
elected; and in 1880 when these committees were
enabled to make byelaws of their own volition.

Many of the school boards and attendance
committees were completely unco-operative, and in
numerous instances they were declared in default,
although this often happened if they were unable
to form a quorum. By 1880, attendance officers had
been appointed in most areas, but as in country
districts they usually held additional posts, their
efficacy was reduced, particularly at seedtime and
harvest. Local authorities were reluctant to
prosecute and magistrates to convict parents who
did not ensure the regular attendance of their
children. A maximum fine of 5/-(20p.) could be
exacted in magistrates' courts, but in practice
penalties were as low as 6d.(2½p.) or 1/-(5p.), sums
which many parents regarded as of little consequence
when counterbalanced with the earnings of their
children. In the 1890s however, there can be no
doubt that the majority of boards and attendance
committees were conscientious in their enforcement
of the educational byelaws, although the penalties
were not raised from 5/- to 20/- until 1900.

The problem of school attendance was unnecessarily
confused by the wide variations in local byelaws.
In 1880 the byelaws of the Education Department which
were applicable in the absence of local schemes,
stipulated that a child who lived more than two
miles from the nearest school need not attend, and
Standards V and III were prescribed respectively for
the total and partial exemption of children over ten
years of age. In practice, 172 local authorities
had a distance excuse of three miles, 403
authorities allowed total exemption of children in
Standard IV; 69 authorities allowed partial
exemption in Standard IV and 90 in Standard II.
Adjoining parishes enforced different standards
when their social and economic conditions could not
justify any variation. In Scotland, on the other
hand, practice was uniform, and a similar pattern
was recommended by the Committee of Council for
England and Wales, without success.(22) In 1902
it was ordered that all children aged five to
fourteen must attend school, but local authorities
could still exempt children of eleven for employment in agriculture, whilst complete or partial
exemption was possible for all children aged twelve
to fourteen.

Until the introduction of compulsory education it was considered that the most influential factor in school attendance was the parents, and the majority of these in 1840 were prepared to withhold their children from school so that they could supplement the family income with their earnings. Children normally attended school until they were old enough to work, and employers frequently claimed that parents entreated them to employ their children as soon as possible. Throughout the evidence given to the Children's Employment Commission in 1862 it was apparent that the children required most protection from their parents.(23)   In areas where agriculture and industry were contiguous, the factory and education laws were abused by parents, for as the minimum age for employment was raised in one sector, the children were encouraged to work in another on which no restriction had been placed.

Throughout the period the earnings of children preserved many working class families from destitution. In the 1840s and 1850s children aged eight and ten could earn a weekly wage of from 2/-(10p) to 8/-(40p) in factories and mines; 2/- or 2/6d. in the Potteries; 4/- or 5/- in agriculture; and 2/6d. as errand boys in London and other large towns. In the 1860s and 1870s boys and girls could earn from 7/- to 12/- in cotton mills, and from 3/- to 4/- in agriculture. The value to the family income of this is clear when it is remembered that in the 1850s and 1860s, adults in cotton mills could earn only 16/- to 28/-, and in agriculture 9/- to 16/-. The standard of living of workmen in London who earned a weekly wage of 21/- in the 1880s was comparatively comfortable, but deteriorated rapidly as their families increased, to improve once more as their children began to work as errand boys and in other permitted occupations. This group of workers represented 14% of the population of East London, and another 20% was even poorer.(24)

Parents did not of course keep their children from school solely on economic grounds. There was an element of active parental hostility to education especially in isolated parts of the country in which attitudes were inherently conservative. The most common cause of educational neglect was however due to apathy on the part of parents. In 1861, 33% of the children who were not at school were said to spend their days in idleness as a result of parental

indifference.(25) In cases where both parents were
employed, the older children were expected to look
after their siblings, and in some parts of the
country, such as Northumberland, the traditional
system of bondagers compelled labourers to provide
a woman for field work, who might be a wife, a
daughter, or a daughter of a neighbour.

A minority of parents was fully aware of the
value of education, and made considerable
sacrifices for their children in this respect.
There were instances before 1870 of parents who
wished to send their children to school, but were
refused permission to do this by their employers.
Other parents, whilst not indifferent to education,
failed to ensure that unwilling children attended
school, but by the end of the century irregular
attendance was confined to a comparatively small
group of children.

The attitude of parents could be influenced to
some extent by the apparent value of education as
manifested in the conditions, curriculum, and
efficiency of schools. For most of the Victorian
period, many parents must surely have held a poor
opinion of the educational system, and could not
reasonably be expected to value it highly. After
1870 it was observed that parents began to take a
pride in the "scraps of new learning acquired by
their children".(26) Not until the 1890s however
was there widespread evidence that schools were
becoming increasingly attractive, teachers
efficient and influential, and local authorities
conscientious, to an extent which would impress a
generation of parents who had not benefited from
this situation. There was conclusive proof that
whenever efficient instruction was provided in
schools, the attendance was good, and even when
depression or a labour dispute reduced the parents
to a state of economic distress, every endeavour
was made to keep the children at school. When the
quality of instruction improved in schools where it
had been badly organized, the level of attendance
usually rose. This was exemplified in a poor
district of London in 1894, when a change of staff
at the local school was followed by a rise in the
average attendance from 70% to 90%, a level which
was maintained.(27)

Attendance at school was sometimes prolonged when
parents were convinced that the prospects of their
children would be likely to improve accordingly. In

1853, the school at Hanley retained a minority of its boys longer than any other in the Potteries. Boys who remained longer at school were engaged afterwards in packing and storing goods, and as clerical assistants, for which they received 4/- (20p) per week, whilst other children earned only 2/- or 2/6d.

The interest of parents in the education of their children was however governed by their financial circumstances. Although secondary education became available to a limited extent after 1890, in practice, large numbers of parents were unable to take advantage of it and intelligent children frequently won scholarships which they could not accept. Even if they actually commenced their studies at secondary school, there was no guarantee that they would remain there for a length of time which would be of permanent benefit to them, and many left at fourteen.

The attitude to education of employers, though less significant than that of parents, was nevertheless important. In the 1830s and 1840s many mine and factory owners were sufficiently aware of their callous attitude to be reluctant to admit that children began to work in their pits and mills as early as seven years old, and sometimes earlier; (28) and there were continuous complaints from clergy and school managers of the antagonism of employers to education. In the Potteries, there were more children aged six to eight who were employed in unhealthy occupations than in any other district in England in the 1850s. The employers did not attempt to justify the morality of this situation, but claimed its necessity in view of the competition with which they had to contend. For most of the period, a large, if not the largest group in the population was, as has been indicated, employed in agriculture, and farmers were notorious for their prolonged opposition to education and evasion of the law. They feared the extension of education as a threat to their supremacy and it was not unknown for parents to be threatened with dismissal if they withdrew their children from labour. As a class, the farmers contributed nothing to the maintenance of local schools prior to 1870, and in the 1880s and 1890s they sat on school boards and attendance committees, and blatantly contravened their own byelaws.

A small minority of employers in all districts
took an active interest in educational provision,
both by generous subscriptions and by personal
influence. In the 1840s the South Hetton Mining
Company of Durham built a school for boys and girls,
and employed teachers for their instruction; and
various mine owners in Northumberland established
schools and provided funds for their upkeep.
Leading manufacturers in the iron districts and
Potteries of the West Midlands in the 1850s claimed
to support the extension of factory legislation to
their industries, and mine owners in Durham stated
their preference for machinery as opposed to child
labour, but did not wish to antagonise the parents!
Farmers claimed that parents stipulated that the
employment of older children must be accompanied by
that of their siblings, but this is not surprising
when the low wages of agricultural labourers is
considered. It is true that these apparently liberal
sentiments may have been voiced with the knowledge
that action was not intended; but as has been seen,
employers began to recognize the potential benefits
of a literate working class when the inferiority of
English manufactures was exposed, and when the
franchise was extended to the artisans in 1867.
Towards the end of the century, many farmers
appeared to be more favourable to education and less
obstructive than in earlier years, and to some
extent this can be attributed to the organization
of vacations to coincide with the seasons of seedtime and harvest.

Employers played a prominent part in Prize Schemes
which were initiated in some industrial areas during
the three decades after 1840. H. Seymour Tremenheere,
the first Inspector of Schools, introduced them into
mining districts between 1843 and 1849, and awarded
ornamental certificates to successful candidates.(29)
The intention was to encourage teachers in their
endeavours and to induce parents to allow their
children to remain at school for a longer period,
and candidates were usually boys aged eleven and
over, who had attended government inspected schools
regularly for at least two years. Schools in large
districts were examined annually in writing,
arithmetic, and recitation, for prizes subscribed by
employers and other local dignitaries, in such areas
as Staffordshire, where in the 1850s children were
removed from instruction at an earlier age than in

any other English county. Other counties in which
these activities took place included the mining
districts of Cheshire, Shropshire, Derbyshire,
Leicestershire, and Nottinghamshire. The prizes
were awarded to successful candidates in the
presence of parents, teachers, local clergy, and
the principal manufacturers and mine owners of the
area.

Opinions varied as to the value of Prize Schemes.
Tremenheere witnessed the pride with which his
certificates were displayed in the homes of prize
winners, and the encouragement they gave to other
members of the family to do likewise. There can be
no doubt that the schemes resulted in children
remaining at school longer than they would normally
have done. However, projects of this kind were very
expensive in terms of the relatively small number
of children who were involved, and in spite of
denials, there is evidence that whilst competitors
were trained, the other children were neglected.
The view of less enthusiastic Inspectors was that
only legislation could solve the problem of
attendance, and where education was not desired for
its own sake, long term success was improbable.
Children could earn £7 to £10 per year in Staffordshire in 1860, and a limited number of prizes of £3
and £4 were insufficient compensation for the loss
of such an income.(30)

In the years after 1870, rewards were offered by
schools to encourage attendance, among which were
certificates of merit and the return of fees. These
inducements had a beneficial influence on the
attendance at school of numbers of children, but not
on persistent truants in the interest of whom
education had been made obligatory.

Reference has been made to the formation of ragged
schools for very poor children who were excluded
from National schools. Poverty was always a factor
in non-attendance or irregular attendance at school,
but its importance was disputed by the Newcastle
Commission. It was admitted that in rare instances
excessive poverty prevented parents from sending
their children to school, but more often it was used
as an excuse where the real attitude was one of
indifference.(31) A considerable number of children
in poor neighbourhoods were accustomed to attending
school without shoes or stockings, and in times of

special hardship, were inadequately fed, but in cases where other items of clothing were not available, it was reasonable that they remained at home. Between 1866 and 1872 it was regularly recorded in the log book of a Liverpool school that absenteeism resulted from poor weather conditions, the implication being that the pupils did not possess suitable clothing. It is significant however that of approximately forty such instances, over half related to absences on Mondays and Fridays, a fact which would suggest parental indifference rather than poverty. On the other hand it is unlikely that the distribution of eighty pairs of clogs and stockings would have been undertaken in the winter of 1894 had there not been genuine hardship.(32)

The payment of fees by children was widespread in all but the last decade of the century. In many schools, particularly after 1862, they were the only reliable income, and in uninspected schools, they were frequently the only income. There was a real temptation for teachers to concentrate their attention on children who could pay the fees, whilst the others were excluded.

During the 1830s and 1840s, fees, which were often determined by the number of subjects studied, were usually 1d. or 2d. per week for working class children, but were in some instances as high as 1/6d. In 1855, 75% of children at school in England and Wales were paying up to 2d., although as much as 8d. was demanded in Wesleyan schools where instruction was provided for a more affluent group. The fees usually varied in proportion to the local rates of wages, so that whilst 4d. was considered reasonable in South Staffordshire in the 1850s, it was prohibitive in Dorset. In 1870 the maximum fee which could be exacted was 9d., with the proviso that up to 10% of the children could pay more. At York in 1888, the fees were raised as children progressed through the schools, a factor which discouraged regular attendance by younger pupils, and encouraged parents to withdraw older children as soon as possible. In London at the same period, the fees varied from one district to another according to the financial capacity of the population, and ranged in general from 1d. to 6d. per week. The fees were lowest in Roman Catholic schools where the children were poorest, and highest in Anglican and Wesleyan establishments.

It is difficult to estimate to what extent parent could afford to pay fees. Nassau Senior, the economist, believed that the majority of working people could afford to have their children educated but "that the sacrifice which they must make for that purpose is grieviously under-rated" when the loss of earnings was considered. He quoted cases to prove that some parents were so poor that they could not pay school fees for their children.(33) Reference was made in Chapter 1 to the findings of Seebohm Rowntree, which support Senior's view. If children were absent for one or two days in a week, they were frequently kept at home for the remaining days in order to avoid paying the fee. On the other hand, it was often claimed that parents could affor to pay fees if they wished to do so. After the Lancashire cotton famine in the 1860s, parents who had been accustomed to the payment of fees by relief committees, were unwilling to meet their obligations when conditions improved. Cheapness was frequently the principal consideration of parents choosing a school for their children, and many children were withdrawn by parents from voluntary schools in London after 1870, and sent to board schools where the fees were lower. In contrast to this, some parents sent their children to the voluntary schools, in order to protect them from the "indiscriminate companionship of the board schools".(34)

The inability of some parents to pay school fees was recognized in the Education Act of 1876, which empowered boards of guardians in parishes to do so on their behalf. The depressed condition of the agricultural community rendered this essential to school attendance. The fees of children aged eleven were also paid by the Education Department until they were fourteen, if they obtained a certificate of proficiency and had been regular in attendance. It was necessary for children to have attended on 350 occasions in any two years, but this reasonably generous stipulation was extended to three years in 1879, four years in 1880, and five years in 1881. In 1888 the Department enabled the fees of poor children to be paid by school boards for their own schools, and by boards of guardians for voluntary schools.

Objections to free education were expressed
throughout the period by individuals such as the
Vicar of King's Somborne in the 1840s, the Rev. J.L.
Brereton in 1856, and Professor Laurie of the
University of Edinburgh in 1888; by the Cross
Commission, and by boards of guardians, who were
often extremely hostile to those who applied to them
for aid. It was believed that free education would
undermine parental independence and responsibility.
Exponents of free education were active in the 1850s
in the National Public School Association, and
clauses for the abolition of fees in elementary
schools were included in abortive Bills in 1853 and
1855. Finally, in the Act of 1891, free education
was introduced into elementary schools, and the
improvement in attendance was immediate, particularly
among infants and older children. However, in 1898,
approximately 14% of the 5,000,000 children at school
were still in establishments which had refused the
government fee grant.(35)

Whereas the influence of poverty on school
attendance was thought by some to be exaggerated,
that of sickness could not be disputed. The health
of thousands of children was impaired by the
conditions in which they lived, worked, and were
educated. Children who attended school on a full
time basis were similarly handicapped if in addition
they worked for any length of time. In 1898 there
were known to be 147,349 children thus employed.
Examples were cited of school boys aged twelve who
ran errands and worked on farms for periods ranging
from thirty two to forty two hours per week in
addition to fulfilling the normal attendance at
school.(36) There was also considerable controversy
in educational and medical circles during the 1880s
relating to "over-pressure in schools, and this was
considered by many to be a cause of ill-health among
children.
Epidemics were a frequent cause of absenteeism
from school. It was shown in Chapter 1 that
vaccination was resisted by the working people. After
discussing a letter from the vestry clerk in 1864,
the committee of a school in Liverpool agreed that
the teachers should be instructed to encourage
parents to have their children vaccinated.(37)
Schools were frequently closed during epidemics or
classes were seriously depleted; for example, malnutrition and scarlet fever resulted in the closure

37

of schools in the East End of London in 1868; and schools in Northumberland and Yorkshire were closed to prevent the spread of epidemics in the 1890s. It was not difficult however in some areas for parents to obtain medical certificates for 3d. or 6d., whether or not the children were genuinely ill. Sickness was sometimes claimed to be a cause of absenteeism at a Liverpool school between 1866 and 1873, but in most instances it occurred on Mondays.(38)

In some country districts children were unable to go to school in the winter or at other times when the weather was bad, because the cart tracks were impassable. This was particularly so in the Fens where difficulty was found in building schools at the most accessible positions in catchment areas, and in the North of Yorkshire. In cases where children had to walk more than two miles to school, it has been shown that their non-attendance was excused in the byelaws of the Education Department in 1880, although practice in this respect varied. Until it was possible to provide schools within reasonable distance of children's homes, the climatic factor would continue to operate to the detriment of attendance.

It may be argued that in the provision of educational facilities and in the attendance of children at school, the most significant developments took place prior to 1870, and that the remaining three decades of the century were devoted to an incomplete consolidation of the position. This conclusion must be subject to qualification. The difficulty of attracting the initial 50% of children who were in attendance by 1870 was certainly less than that of reaching the additional 30% who were placed on the registers between 1870 and 1885. Also, the length of school life was only extended appreciably from 1880, and the average daily attendance did not rise above 70% until the 1890s. The value of attendance as an influence on literacy must of necessity be closely related to the efficiency of teachers, the organization of schools, the scope of the curriculum, methods of instruction, and other factors which will be examined during the course of this volume.

REFERENCES

1   The North and South Corporation Schools at
    Liverpool were erected in 1826, and were
    founded and controlled not by a religious
    organization but by the Borough Council.
2   Elementary Education Acts, Final Report(1888)
    p.8.
3   Brown, C.K.F., The church's part in education,
    p.168 and Appendix.
4   Committee of Council on Education, Report(1861),
    p.264.
5   State of Popular Education in England, Report
    (1861), Vol.1, pp.202-6.
6   Senior, N.W., Suggestions on popular education,
    p.187.
7   Ratcliff, C., Ragged schools in relation to the
    government grants for education, p.41.
8   Manchester Statistical Society, Report on the
    state of education in the borough of Liverpool
    in 1835-1836, pp.26-7.
9   Elementary Education Acts, op. cit., p.162.
10 Ibid. p.8.
11 Kay, J., The social condition and education of
    the people, Vol.2, p.502.
12 Ratcliff, C., op. cit., pp.iv-viii, 63.
13 Morley, J., The struggle for national education,
    2nd ed., p.3.
14 Kay-Shuttleworth, J.P.. Public education, pp.3,
    5, 8, 11.
15 Elementary Education Acts, op. cit., p.158.
16 Schools Inquiry Commission, Report(1868), Vol.1,
    pp.79, 82-3, 103.
17 Royal Commission on Secondary Education,
    Report(1895), Vol.1, p.85.
18 Ibid. p.64.
19 State of Popular Education in England, op. cit.,
    Vol.1, p.179; Vol.2, p.461.
20 Committee of Council on Education, Reports,
    1873-1899; Board of Education, Reports,
    1899-1901.
21 Committee of Council on E ucation, Report,
    1897-1898, pp.viii-ix.
22 Ibid. 1880-1881, pp.xxvii-xxviii; 1881-1882,
    pp.xxix-xxxv
23 Children's Employment Commission, Fifth Report
    (1866), p.lliv.
24 Booth, C.(ed), Labour and life of the people,
    Vol.1, pp.33-44, 48-50.

25 State of Popular Education in England, op. cit. Vol.1, p.179.
26 Runciman, J., Schools and scholars, p.27.
27 Committee of Council on Education, op. cit., 1895-1896, p.132.
28 Children's Employment Commission, First report, (1842), p.13; Second Report (1843), pp.7-12.
29 Tremenheere, H.S. I was there, pp.71-2.
30 Committee of Council on Education, op. cit., 1853-1854, Vol.1, 391-418; 1855-1856, p.376; 1859-1860, pp.69-71, 159.
31 State of Popular Education in England, op. cit. Vol.1, pp.178, 179.
32 Liverpool, St. Columba's Mixed School, Diary, 1866-1894.
33 Senior, N.W., op. cit., pp.3-4, 158-60.
34 Booth, C.(ed.), op. cit., Vol.2, p.488.
35 Committee of Council on Education, op. cit., 1898-1899, pp.iv-v.
36 Ibid. pp.x, 242.
37 Liverpool, Benevolent Society and Free School of St. Patrick, Committee book, 28th April 1864.
38 Liverpool, St. Columba's Mixed School, op. cit., pp.80, 83, 85.

3 The Teaching Profession

In the 1830s an efficient organization for the
training of teachers did not exist, and for this
reason most of those who taught in elementary schools
were not equipped to do so. There were in 1836, 244
teachers in Liverpool dame schools of whom only two
claimed to be trained, 192 in common day schools of
whom only eighteen claimed to be trained, and forty
two in charity schools of whom eighteen claimed to
be trained.(1) Teachers in the schools of the
National and British and Foreign Schools Societies
in the 1840s were generally uneducated and untrained,
as were those in Sunday schools. In part of South
London in 1858, of 236 teachers, only 122 had
received any training, and of these, sixty five were
certificated.(2)

Teaching was often practised by men and women who
were otherwise unemployed either through age, ill-
health, or redundancy. The Newcastle Commission
reported that teachers were frequently unemployed
bar maids, domestic servants, lodging house keepers,
milliners, and toy salesmen, many of whom were
consumptive or crippled. Another group taught whilst
they continued to be occupied as journeymen, key-
makers, locksmiths, miners, and small master
craftsmen. Many of them were scarcely literate, and
were quite incapable of exerting a positive

educational influence over the children placed in their care. It is true that a large proportion of these teachers were employed in private schools, but in 1858 these establishments catered for 34% of the children under instruction.(3)

It was claimed that the value of trained teachers was apparent, not only as regards their academic qualities, but also in their ability to impart knowledge to children, although an aptitude for teaching was preferable to erudition. Whilst teachers were normally the only possible contact poor children were likely to have with cultural values, the steps which were taken after 1839 to improve their qualifications were quite inadequate, and the problem was never solved in public element- ary schools during the 19th century. This is demonstrated in the following statistics from reports of the Committee of Council on Education:

	Untrained Male Teachers %	Untrained Female Teachers %
1875	24	37
1884	31	52
1888	32	55
1894	29	51
1898	29	51

The reason for the almost continuous increase in the proportion of untrained teachers was due to the facilities which existed for study for certificates on a part-time basis. Between 1871 and 1884, certificates were granted without examination to over one thousand male, and almost two thousand female teachers who were untrained, but on whose schools the Inspectors had reported favourably. This facility was withdrawn in the Code of 1885, but the fact remains that the demand for teachers during the fifteen years after 1870 could not have been met without the availability of untrained staff. In the Code of 1890 it was intended to reduce the number of untrained teachers by raising the standard of the examinations, but as the figures show, the fall was not significant between 1888 and 1898.

Although untrained teachers were usually condemned by Inspectors, there were exceptions throughout the period who were considered competent. There were instances of masters who, aware of their inadequacy recommenced their education. A writer commented in in 1862 that some of the best teachers had the poorest certificates, whilst many of the most successful were uncertificated.(4) In Somerset in 1865 several of the untrained teachers were superior to many who had been trained, in ability, zeal, and practical success, but the Inspector confessed that he seldom left such schools "without regretting that a person of such ability had not had the additional advantage of training".(5) The Cross Commission commented in 1888 that "there are some persons with a natural aptitude for teaching who have not entered training colleges, but who could not be excluded from the profession without a real loss to our schools".(6) It is true however, that a considerable proportion of the untrained teachers were unqualified only in the sense that they had not attended a training college. They had been engaged as pupil-teachers under the supervision of highly qualified heads in large schools prior to their success in the examination for certificates. From 1865 no school could qualify for a Government grant unless the head teacher was certificated.

Prior to 1840, teachers who organized their schools according to the system of mutual instruction were necessarily assisted by monitors who were selected from the more proficient pupils, and each of whom would instruct a class which varied in size from eight to twelve children in British schools and from twelve to thirty in National schools. Inspectors between 1839 and 1846 found that this system was not a success owing to the inadequate knowledge and technical ineptitude of the monitors. Thus it was abolished as far as possible, and in 1846 a five year apprenticeship of pupil-teachers aged at least thirteen was introduced. By this means it was hoped to strengthen the teaching staff of schools and to provide for a continual supply of suitable candidates for training, who were expected to pass an examination for a certificate. Numerous young people left their existing occupations and returned to school as a result of the Minute of 1846, but a large proportion of pupil-teachers did not proceed to the training colleges after they were certificated. Financial inducements were offered to candidates, who were known as Queen's Scholars, in 1846 and 1855, in order to encourage them to undergo formal training, and Queen's Scholarships were awarded for the first time in 1852. By 1860 a large majority of the pupil-teachers successfully completed their apprenticeship; and over 75% became candidates for, and usually obtained, Queen's Scholarships. In the 1870s however, many potential students were unable to enter college owing to inadequate accommodation.

Apprentices received one hour and a half of elementary instruction each day, which was followed by a similar period in which lessons were prepared, and during a further five hours they became familiar with the arts of school management and teaching, by being placed in charge of a class. The committee of Council envisaged that in contrast the course at training college should be primarily concerned with the acquisition of academic ability, but some Inspectors thought that in practice the course was designed to exercise their memories rather than to develop their intelligence. Pupil-teachers could only be engaged in schools which were under inspection, adequately provided with books and apparatus, and in the charge of competent teachers who were remunerated for the additional work which was entailed. In instances were head teachers were not sufficiently qualified to instruct pupil-teachers, a temporary expedient was to engage Stipendiary Monitors for four years, who received less advanced instruction than was normal for pupil-teachers.

Rudimentary as the apprenticeship of pupil-teachers was, it was seriously undermined by the Revised Code of 1862 which discontinued grants and reduced the number of apprentices which could be engaged. This resulted in a significant diminution in the numbers of young people entering apprenticeships, and who in the 1860s benefited in other occupations from the general rise in wages which occurred at that time. In addition, teachers frequently preferred to economise by not appointing apprentices. Fortunately the decline in the number of pupil-teachers was short term and was arrested in 1867, in which year a recovery was observed in some areas, but not in all. It is possible however, that the return to teaching was directly related to the economic depression of 1867-9. The Education Department was not eager to encourage a revival in the supply of pupil-teachers, and limited their number in schools to three for each certificated teacher in 1877, and to one additional pupil-teacher for each certificated assistant teacher in 1882.

In practice the pupil-teacher system had defects. Scholars who were chosen for apprenticeship were usually very young, frequently poorly educated, and consequently ill-equipped initially to teach. As after 1870 the Committee of Council could impose a fine if the number of teachers was too few for the children in attendance, the managers were often obliged to engage almost any pupil of sufficient age who was willing to be apprenticed for the five year period. Also, the head teachers were frequently inadequately qualified, and there was evidence that in some cases, pupil-teachers, required more thorough tuition in the teaching of reading. The pupil-teacher organization was attacked by the Cross Commission as "the weakest part of the educational system", and many teachers advocated its abolition. (7)

In the course of their daily programme, the pupil-teachers were considered by many to be overworked, with adverse effects on their health, which was likely to undermine their subsequent efficiency as teachers. Although their Saturdays were free, the eight hour working day from Monday to Friday was too long for boys and girls aged sixteen and seventeen. For this reason it was approved by many educationists that whilst in 1861 pupil-teachers comprised 63% of the teaching profession, in 1885 the proportion had decreased to 30%. Candidates had to provide a certificate of good health from school managers after 1862, and for their protection the requirements were more closely defined at intervals between 1870 and the end of the century. In a report to the Department in 1884, Dr. J. Crichton-Browne claimed that shortly after the commencement of their apprenticeship many manifested evidence of ill-health which deteriorated as they progressed through the course. In contrast, J.G. Fitch, a prominent H.M.I., commented that certificates of good health were all too easily obtainable by pupil-teachers, and he claimed that the work could be undertaken "with perfect ease by any youth or maiden in ordinary health who has a liking for teaching and for intellectual pursuits". (8) Supporters of the system emphasized that without it there could never have been sufficient qualified teachers in elementary schools, and that England had "a better and more abundant supply of trained teachers than any country in Europe". (9) The period of apprenticeship was reduced in 1878 from five to four years, and in 1899 to three years.

In various ways the pupil-teacher system was rendered more effective after 1870. Several school boards improved the training facilities of pupil-teachers by the establishment of centres at which they were taught by experts. Examples of this kind were to be found in London in 1875 and Liverpool in 1876, but not until the 1890s had central classes been set up by school boards and voluntary bodies in almost every part of England. In this way the efficiency of the pupil-teacher system was improved, although in 1898 candidates were still insufficiently prepared for admission to training colleges. The London scheme necessitated attendance in the evening hours at first, which only resulted in increased over-pressure, but in 1884 it was arranged that half of the school day should be spent in school and the other half at the centre. Pressure was eased too in Liverpool, where in 1883 all pupil-teachers in board schools were allowed one half day per week in school hours for private study, and in 1884 all first year pupil-teachers were made half-timers. As a result of these changes the pupil-teachers were more success-ful in the scholarship examination than in places which did not operate schemes of this kind. The Cross Commission favoured the availability of more time for private study,(10) and in a Memorandum to Inspectors in 1891, the Committee of Council approved the establishment of central classes. The Code of 1890 was designed to ensure that the training of pupil-teachers became more efficient, by the stipulation that the apprenticeship was only satisfactorily completed after success in the Queen's Scholarship Examination, and by reserving until the last year a special grant to assist the candidates on their commencement at training college. Although pupil-teachers continued to be largely drawn from elementary schools, it became increasingly common towards the end of the century for them to be engaged from secondary schools. After 1896 they could be apprenticed if they had been successful in the Oxford Local examination for junior students, the Certificate Examination of the College of Preceptors, or any similar examination approved by the Education Department. After 1897 pupil-teachers could not be apprenticed until they were fifteen years of age.

Prior to the formation of training colleges, the religious bodies employed organizing masters, who

46

visited schools in order to advise teachers as to the adoption of the most effective organization and methods. In 1839 an Archidiaconal Board was established at Leicester to ascertain the most appropriate means of making existing teachers more efficient, and in 1841 a summer school was planned, which did not take place owing to a lack of funds. Instead, the Board requested an organizing master from the National Society, who visited a number of schools in the area. The British and Foreign School Society on the other hand possessed a central school at Borough Road in London, which had been founded by Joseph Lancaster in 1805, and teachers for its schools were trained there until 1842. In 1835 the National Society had two central schools at Westminster and forty three in the provinces. Students were trained for short periods, for example, the course organized by the Home and Colonial School Society in 1836 lasted for twelve weeks, but was extended to fifteen weeks in 1838.

The government wished to establish a state controlled Normal School, and granted £10,000 for the purpose in 1835, but so great was the opposition from ecclesiastical circles that the project was abandoned. In 1840 a college was founded at Battersea by James Kay-Shuttleworth, which was a success and was transferred to the National Society four years later. In 1844 the government recommended that the allocation granted in 1835 for the erection of normal schools should be divided equally between the National and British Societies, although grants for maintenance were not provided until 1846. Between 1839 and 1847, thirteen colleges were established in England, and after the introduction of maintenance grants the movement received fresh impetus in the formation of one by the Wesleyans in 1851, and two by the Roman Catholics in 1854 and 1856. By 1858, twenty nine colleges in England constituted what was to be the main contribution by the voluntary bodies to teacher training in the 19th century, and later endeavours were confined principally to the improvement of existing colleges. In 1868 there were thirty voluntary colleges in England, thirty six in 1875, thirty seven in 1879, thirty nine in 1888, and forty one in 1898. It was estimated however that forty one colleges were necessary in 1850, (11) a sad commentary on the inadequacy of training facilities in the Victorian period.

47

The government decided to withhold further grants towards the erection of normal schools in 1859, but they were reintroduced after strong opposition from the voluntary bodies, differing however, in that they were made retrospective rather than prospective as had been the case since 1844. In 1859 the state contributed 76% of the total income for maintaining male colleges, and 71% for female colleges, in most, but not all of which, income exceeded expenditure. The proportion granted by the government was 71% in 1865 and 72.6% in 1887. Conditions were frequently unsatisfactory in the colleges, and one men's college was likened to "the common room of a work-house".(12) Major improvements were made in the voluntary colleges after 1890 when the Day colleges were commenced under the auspices of universities and university colleges. In 1898 there were thirteen Day colleges in England together with the forty one voluntary establishments to which reference has been made.

The output of the colleges was never adequate for the increased numbers of children who were at school In the years prior to 1870 the colleges were seldom fully occupied. Great difficulty was encountered in obtaining candidates in the 1840s, and the Rev. Henry Moseley, H.M.I., reported in 1853 that although the fourteen male colleges inspected by him could accommodate 855 students, the total number in residence was 489. Two factors contributed to a lack of demand in the 1860s: the economic boom which encouraged young people to enter more remunerative occupations without preliminary training, and the increase in fees and reduction in grants enforced by the Revised Code. In 1865 the colleges could accommodate 2,500 students but only 1,822 were in residence. The situation improved after 1870, and in 1877, whilst the total accommodation was sufficient for 3,111 students, 3,027 were in residence. Eventually the colleges were unable to cope with the demand, and in 1886, whilst 3,379 candidates passed the entrance examination, only 1,682 were given places. 1,045 men who were suitably qualified, offered themselves for training in 1897, and 980 were accepted, whilst the applications of 1,194 women were rejected.

The absence of facilities for the training of infant teachers was a major defect in the educational system. Samuel Wilderspin stressed the need in 1835 for a central establishment for this purpose,(13) and in 1839 the Inspectors were asked to ascertain if teachers had undergone specific instruction in infant education. In 1836 the Home and Colonial Infant School Society was founded, and in 1854 a Minute of the Committee of Council encouraged training colleges to organize courses for students who wished to become teachers in infant schools. However, in 1859 only thirty two students per year were specially prepared for the task, and the urgency of the situation was emphasized once more in the report of the Newcastle Commission.(14) Not until 1884 did the British and Foreign School Society found its college at Saffron Walden for the training of infant teachers.

A continuing obstacle to the growth of literacy was the social class from which the students were drawn. The first students at Battersea in 1840 were pauper children from the industrial school at Norwood, and the Committee of Council complained in the 1850s that the training colleges were occupied by students of the lower class who were culturally deprived and were not suitably adapted to training. The Cross Commission expressed the view that the results of training were exemplary when the "very poor quality" of students was considered.(15) Students from working class homes were unable to acquire a liberal education even if they wished to do so, for during their teens they were, as has been shown, occupied for long hours in learning and teaching the rudiments of elementary education. The training colleges could only partially counter-balance these disadvantages "which economic conditions had made inevitable".(16)

The Committee of Council was aware of the need for suitable candidates, and in the 1840s clergymen and managers of schools were asked to "select from such as are personally known to them, promising youths, with whom those training colleges might be filled".(17) In the Code of 1882, an attempt was made to encourage graduates of universities and women who had passed university examinations, to become teachers in elementary schools, but during a period of six years, not one application was made. In effect, the Code of 1882 would have resulted in individuals of cultural and academic distinction taking up teaching without an understanding of educational method. This was corrected in 1896,when graduates were expected to possess a certificate of proficiency in the theory and practice of teaching

obtained at a Day training college. Although there
was no pronounced influx of graduates into elementary schools, there was evidence after 1870 that the
social background of students had improved. In 1896
a survey of a training college for women in London
revealed that of 94 students, nine were daughters
of teachers, seventeen of clerks, five of civil
servants, two of farmers, and six of engineers. In
a male college of 93 students, a similar analysis
was obtained, and it was thought probable that a
survey of students in other colleges would confirm
this pattern.(18)   Between 1870 and 1900 the social
background of elementary school teachers improved
appreciably, most of them having been educated in
elementary schools, but representing a "distinctly
higher and more intelligent clas" than formerly.(19)

As has been seen, the course in the central school
of the religious bodies before 1840 lasted for a few
weeks at a time, but the Committee of Council
envisaged that those in training colleges would be
attended for up to three years. In practice the
course at Battersea in 1847 lasted for one year. The
Minutes of 1846 made it clear that a course of three
years was contemplated, but no adequate encouragemen
was given to students to extend their period of
training. However, in 1853 it was stipulated that th
grants of £20 to £30 which were made to colleges
according to the class obtained by the students in
the examinations, would be withheld from all who did
not remain for a second year. For a brief period, an
exception was made to this ruling, so that colleges
could also receive a grant of £10 for students who
remained for an additional six months after the firs
year. At Borough Road it was claimed that the demand
for women teachers was so great that the committee
was unable to retain any for a second year. As a
result of the Minute of 1853 the two year course was
more widely adopted, but that of three year duration
found little support. In 1859 there were two third
year students at St. Mark's; and in 1884, of 15,863
male teachers, none had trained for more than two
years. The Cross Commission proposed that the course
should be extended to three years for a selected
number of students who would be likely to benefit.(2
In the 1890s the third year was made compulsory in
some of the Day colleges, and wherever it was
introduced, the cultural background of those involve
was said to be considerably improved. Until 1890 the
social status of students rendered it necessary for

50

hem to reside in the colleges "in order that they
ay be constantly under the eye of the rector...and
eparated from injurious influences".(21) It is
erhaps a reflection of the improvement in the class
f candidates that the Day colleges were opened, and
acilities offered to non-residents in voluntary
olleges.

The concept of residential colleges was ideal if
he students were to be assisted in their cultural
evelopment. It was important that the staff of the
olleges should be able to contribute to the growth
f literacy in those who were being trained. During
he five decades after 1840, the staff of training
olleges was generally reported as being efficient,
nd even excellent, although an observer in 1872
ommented that at one college the governesses were
orking class in origin, and the majority consisted
f former students of the establishment.(22)   An
nspector in 1888 confirmed that many of the earlier
eports were not sufficiently objective, and stated
hat there had been "a steady improvement in the
ualifications of the teaching staff", which still
ncluded, in many instances, former students.(23)
imilar statements were made in the reports for
891 and 1895, with the rider that numerous
raduates had been appointed. Where former students
ere appointed in the 1890s, they were generally
rawn from those who had been trained for three
ears, with an additional course at colleges in
rance, Germany, or Switzerland.

It is true that the students would only be
expected to teach children to a low standard, as
ill be seen in Chapter 5. However, although much of
the twelve month course at Battersea in the 1840s
as spent in teaching students to read, write, and
spell, an extremely superficial knowledge was also
equired on nineteen different subjects. Courses at
ther men's colleges were similar, and the Newcastle
Commission complained that "the public money is not
oted in order to give a certain number of young
ersons a sort of academic education" in subjects,
any of which were not at that time taught in
elementary schools. The Commissioners advocated an
academic course confined to reading, arithmetic,
English history, geography, chemistry, and one other
physical or applied science. This criticism did not
apply to women's colleges in which the curriculum
consisted solely of subjects taught in elementary
schools, increasing in difficulty in the second

year.(24) In 1862 the training college syllabus was
reduced "almost to the level that might be attained
by a really clever boy in the first class of a good
National school". Some colleges continued to provide
a wider syllabus than that required of them, but
gradually they were forced to curtail their
activities as pupil-teachers began to commence their
courses equipped only with an elementary knowledge
of the basic subjects. In 1872 the syllabus in
training colleges was almost the same as it had been
in 1862.(25)

T.H. Huxley, the eminent scientist and a founder
member of the London School Board, criticized those
who believed "that elementary teaching might be
properly carried out by teachers provided with only
elementary knowledge";(26) but after 1870 such
criticisms were increasingly met as the curriculum
in schools was gradually widened, and by 1876 the
syllabuses in both men's and women's colleges
included a larger number of subjects. Failures in
examinations were unusual, although in 1880 many
students showed an inability to write an essay. In
1891 a new syllabus was introduced in which the
course for each year was divided into two parts, the
first was obligatory, and academic subjects consisted
of reading, repetition, and writing; and the second,
all other subjects. The most promising students were
given facilities to read for the matriculation
examination of the University of London, and in some
colleges all students were entered for the examination, so that those who remained at college for three
years could graduate before they left.

The requirements of the syllabus in reading in 1859
which applied to both colleges for men and women, was
as follows:

First Year To read with a distinct utterance,
with due attention to punctuation and with just
expression, a passage from Mr. Warren's "Select
Extracts from Blackstone's Commentaries".

Moseley appears to have been responsible for the use
of this work, and in a letter to the Lord President
he commented that "the style of Blackstone is so
remarkable for purity, for simplicity, and for
strength, that no better book could probably be
selected as a prose reading lesson-book in the first
years' course".(27)

Second Year To read with a distinct utterance,

with due attention to the punctuation and a
just expression, a passage from Milton's
"Paradise Lost" or from Shakspeare(sic).

n 1869 the syllabus was amended and first year
tudents were expected

To read a passage in prose, and another in
verse, with a distinct utterance, due
attention to the punctuation and just
expression.

he syllabus for second year students made greater
emands on their ability than previously:

Candidates will be expected to show improvement
in the higher qualities of reading, such as
expression, modulation of voice, and the correct
delivery of long or involved sentences.

t that time a repetition exercise was included in
he reading examination, a situation which persisted
hroughout the 19th century.

In 1878 the first year syllabus was amended
lightly so that it was no longer necessary to read
 particular form of literature, but emphasis was
till placed on utterance, punctuation, and
xpression, and in 1896 the second year syllabus was
hrased in the same terms. The last amendment in
he Victorian period occurred in 1898, from which
ate it was stipulated that both first and second
ear students were "to read with ease and precision".

From 1879 it was specified that students would be
xamined in their ability to read particular works.
n that year first year students read a passage from
cott's Marmion, Byron's Childe Harold, and
acaulay's Historical Essays; and second year
tudents from Shakespeare's The Tempest and Macbeth,
ohnson's Lives of the poets, and from a newspaper.
t was directed that the works concerned "must not
e studied in class, but must be left to the private
eading of the students". The set books, of which a
ear's notice was given, were varied each year to
nclude different works by the same authors or
riters of similar standing, and from 1884 passages
rom only two works were required. The reading of a
ewspaper became an alternative rather than an
bligatory requirement in the second year from 1884,
nd from 1887 its use was discontinued. From 1888
ach student was examined from one of the books
rescribed for his year and from one other book

chosen by the Inspector without notice. The
insistence on students being examined in their
ability to read from books with which they were not
familiar was a development which removed any
opportunity for them to memorize passages as had fo
many years been the practice in schools. The
newspaper had of course served the same purpose. A
test of this kind was effective provided the
Inspector chose a suitable book for the examination
In 1898 particular titles ceased to be specified at
all and tests were carried out "from any two books
approved beforehand by the Inspector", in addition
to another book brought or chosen by him.

Although prospective teachers could reasonably be
expected to satisfy the requirements in reading
without difficulty this was not the case. In his
report on the college at Battersea in 1845, Moseley
was highly critical of the students' performance in
reading:

> I regret not to be able to express a
> favourable opinion of the success with which
> this important element in the course of
> instruction proper to a training school has
> been pursued. Where the period of instruc-
> tion is so limited, and the knowledge to be
> acquired so extensive and so varied, but
> little leisure can be left for the
> acquisition of reading. (28)

At another college in 1847 the examination in
reading was not characterized by correct emphasis o
just expression, and in some cases was defective in
mechanical facility and utterance, yet on the whole
there was an improvement in these respects as
compared with former examinations.(29) In the same
year only 49% of students at St. Mark's, Chelsea
obtained a Grade A pass in reading, compared with
75% in writing and 74% in Greek. During the 1850s
and 1860s women students tended to be superior in
their reading ability to men, and whilst the result
of the former were increasingly graded as "Excellen
or "Good", the latter were usually "Fair". The
situation was generally reversed after 1870, and in
1875, for example, only 52% of the first year and
71% of the second year students in men's colleges
obtained 60% or more in the reading and repetition
examination; whilst the equivalent percentages in
the women's colleges were 51 and 62.

The following percentages give an indication of t

give an indication of the reading and recitative ability of students in the voluntary colleges as evidenced in examinations in the 1880s and 1890s:

	Male		Female	
	First Year	Second Year	First Year	Second Year
1881	69	71	69	67
1884	69	75	70	72
1888	72	73	69	71
1891	72	73	71	74
1894	68	70	73	75
1898	72	76	79	80

Although a gradual improvement in reading is apparent, particularly in the women's colleges, it is necessary to observe that a pass percentage of 75% was not attained in any category until 1884 and one of 80% until 1898. It is a sad commentary on the educational system of this country that so many student teachers not only entered college but also completed their courses and took posts in schools whilst they were at best semi-literate. On the other hand there is no way of isolating the students' performance in reading from that in recitation, and it is possible that the students were more superior in their ability to read than to memorize passages from books. Average passes in reading in Day colleges were marginally lower than those in residential institutions in the late 1890s.

For most of the Victorian period particular concern was expressed that insufficient attention was given in colleges to the art of teaching. This included not only all matters which related to the organization of schools, such as the arrangement of desks, size of classes, and compilation of time-tables, but also the manner in which knowledge was imparted to the children. In the latter instance, much depended on the aptitude of students for their vocation. Moseley complained continually between 1848 and 1855 that trained teachers did not teach as well as was necessary, (30) and even in 1884 it was reported that the proportion of time devoted to management was still neglected in colleges, though not as much as in earlier years. Lectures in school management were common from the 1850s, and it was included in the syllabus of 1876, but very few staff were involved, except at the Home and Colonial College and at Warrington. In the 1880s however, considerable improvement was observed in the teaching ability of students in a number of colleges, whilst

at the same time it remained unsatisfactory in other
School management was included in the obligatory
section of the syllabus of 1891, and the Committee
of Council insisted that all students should be
adequately trained in techniques.

Practising and model schools were attached to many
colleges by 1853, and indeed this principle was
underlined in 1839. The former made students aware
of the situation as it existed in schools, whilst th
latter represented an ideal organization. At first
students worked in practising schools for part of
each day, or for more concentrated periods towards
the end of the course; or, as in the male department
at Borough Road in 1859, for two weeks at a time. In
1865 every first year student at Borough Road spent
four weeks in the practising school, and every
second year student, two. The widespread practice in
the 1880s was for a total period of three weeks to
be spent in school, the first being for observation.
Throughout the period there was general approval of
the school practice system, and failures were sometimes attributed to an absence of practising
facilities. In 1884 the practising schools were
reported as efficient in various institutions, but
none was available at such places as Cheltenham,
Ripon, and Salisbury.

Moseley was an early critic of the system which he
considered artificial, aiming as it did to divide
the school into as many classes as possible to meet
the needs of more students than could be adequately
trained.(31) The complaint that there were too few
children in the practising schools was made of
Bishop's Stortford College in 1880, where there were
157 children and sixty students. A similar situation
existed at Bristol, Chichester, and Lincoln; and
Canon Warburton, H.M.I., considered practising
schools in the 1880s as so inadequate that students
should be sent to well organized schools in the area
which were not attached to the colleges.(32) This
was not in fact a new idea, and had been pioneered
at Borough Road in 1859, but it became more popular
in the 1880s and 1890s. The Day training colleges
used ordinary schools with good local reputations.
In defence of the attached practising schools, it
was claimed that they were nearly always as
efficiently organized as was possible in spite of
such deficiencies as obsolete buildings, and the

demands of an increasing number of student teachers. Improvements were effected in many schools after 1895, but it is also true that they were often "miserably furnished with old-fashioned rickety desks;...ill-equipped with proper apparatus; gloomy and dingy". Much of the time spent in these schools was wasted, because in them the students reverted to the "fossilized routines they were accustomed to in their own schools", and saw nothing of progressive educational method.(33)

After 1850 it became increasingly the custom for colleges with more than sixty students to appoint a master of method who was concerned with instruction in organization and teaching techniques. By 1880 nearly all colleges had established a post of this kind. It was regarded as preferable for the master of method to supervise the students during school practice rather than the mistress of the school, although where the practising facilities were located at a distance from the college, as at Salisbury in the 1850s, it was difficult to realize this policy. The role of supervisor was transferred slowly from school mistress to expert, and in 1872 weekly reports were still sent from the mistress of the practising school attached to Warrington College to the master of method, who was not involved in the supervision of students. It was difficult for any master of method, unassisted, to supervise students distributed in several schools, although the problem was reduced where the students were observing rather than teaching.

In both academic and technical courses, the students were until after 1880 expected to attend a large number of lectures, and were not given sufficient opportunity for private study. "Life for them shrank into a sordid round of mean hopes, mean rivalries, mean struggles, sapless, joyless efforts to grasp worthless knowledge".(34) Criticism was made of the library facilities in the 1850s and later. The library at Cheltenham Men's College in the 1870s was described as "a standing joke, and but rarely used". At another college there was a lack of privacy and "it was hardly possible to read out of class hours". The introduction of Day colleges after 1890 acted as a stimulant to the voluntary bodies, many of whose colleges had grown moribund in their aims and methods. Libraries were among the features which were improved, and day rooms were

introduced, which were likely to encourage reading.
None had existed prior to 1886, but by 1898 the
colleges in which they were not provided were
exceptions.(35) However, if colleges were
inadequately provided with books, apart from texts,
the poor cultural attainments of students were
unlikely to be improved. If students were unaccustomed to using books, it is unlikely that as teacher
they would encourage their pupils to do so.

It has been shown that although the output of the
colleges was never adequate for the ever increasing
numbers of children who were at school, teachers
who had been trained were supplemented by a
substantial number of men and women who had not
undergone a course of training. It is important
therefore to ascertain whether there were in fact
sufficient teachers of all kinds to instruct the
children in elementary schools. At no time of course
were there sufficient infant teachers. The Manchester
Statistical Society in its survey of education in
Liverpool in 1836, reported that there was no class
of competent teachers in existence,(36) but
gradually a teaching force was organized. Prior to
1870 there were never sufficient teachers, and as
has been seen, many withdrew from the profession
after 1862. There was a particular scarcity of male
teachers, but by 1880 the supply was considered
adequate. One training college principal wrote to
the Education Department expressing fear that
students leaving college would find difficulty in
obtaining suitable posts. In order to attract
teachers after 1870 standards had been relaxed, but
there was no doubt in 1888 that they must once more
be raised before supply exceeded demand. For many
years it had been calculated that the annual wastage
was approximately 6%, but when the withdrawals which
took place in the years 1882-1886 were analysed it
was discovered that the wastage was only 3.3%. The
demand for women teachers continued in the 1880s,
but in contrast to the 1860s there was a surplus of
men. The number of certificated teachers rose from
6,393 in 1860 to 12,676 in 1870, and 42,212 in 1886;
and the number of uncertificated teachers rose from
7,652 in 1880 to 17,439 in 1886.

The superfluity of teachers must however be
questioned, relating as it did to the pupil/staff
ratios which obtained in elementary schools. After

1870 the Education Department ruled that in towns there must be a head and four pupil-teachers in a school of two hundred boys. In practice teachers in London board schools were each expected to teach sixty children, and sometimes two classes simultaneously. There were in 1891 some board schools in which classes of seventy or eighty children were not uncommon, and sometimes ninety or one hundred were taught by one certificated and one pupil-teacher. Sydney Buxton, the Liberal politician, referred to an instance in a voluntary school where one teacher was in charge of a school of sixty eight children divided into six Standards. He drew the conclusion that over-pressure among teachers was due to insufficient establishments in schools, but was subjective in his claim that the voluntary schools were the principal culprits.(37) Teachers in urban areas tended to have too many children to control, whilst those in rural districts had a smaller number of pupils divided into five or six Standards with which they frequently coped without assistance. It was more difficult to obtain staff in rural than in urban schools. In contrast to the situation of over-pressure, Standards VI and VII were usually quite small, and it would probably have been more economical to have grouped older children from a specified catchment area in a school specially prepared for the purpose. It is clear that if the distribution of teachers had been more efficiently organized, and classes reduced to a more realistic size, there need never have been any employment problems in the teaching profession.

The difficulty of obtaining teachers between 1830 and 1880 must be related to the inducements which were offered for suitable candidates to make teaching their vocation. The status of the profession in the community must be considered. It is natural that the calibre of teachers, as described earlier, would not command respect in the community, although many by their own efforts improved their qualifications. Pupil-teachers were drawn, with rare exceptions, from the most respectable families among the working class in their parishes, and were considered more suitable for their task than more wealthy individuals who regarded the occupation with condescension. In general however, schoolmasters in the 1840s and 1850s were thought of as appendages of the parochial system. The Principal

of Battersea College in the 1840s believed the
status of the teacher was improving, but declared
that "he is an educated peasant, living among the
peasantry, sympathising with their wants and
pursuits, and endeavouring to lead them in whatever
promotes their civilization".(38) In 1850, Joseph
Kay doubted whether well educated men would be
tempted "to engage in such a despised...profession"
when they could obtain a livelihood as tradesmen.(39)
However, by 1861 the Newcastle Commission was able
to report that teachers were "universally regarded
as respectable and useful", if not the social equals
of surgeons and lawyers.(40) After 1870 the social
position of teachers appears to have advanced, and
this may be attributed partially to the work of
colleges into which they entered "raw, self-
conscious, and awkward" and emerged "capable and
self-possessed". The decreased rate of wastage in
the 1880s could reasonably be traced to improved
social status; and in contrast to the inferior role
of teachers hitherto, a writer in 1879 described
them as belonging to a "deserving profession", but
who had "rather an exaggerated idea of their own
importance".(41) James Runciman, an educational
journalist, condemned Charles Dickens, whose
caricatures of teachers, he claimed, had brought the
profession into disrepute; and also the training
college courses which produced teachers whose
inferiority was such that they must "endure the
mockery of cultured folk".(42)

In addition to a desire for social status, "there
can be no doubt that views of personal advancement
have as much influence upon teachers throughout
their whole career as upon other persons".(43) It
is interesting therefore to examine the salaries
which were commanded by teachers during the
Victorian period.

1837-1850 The Committee of Council in 1839
considered that the salaries of teachers should be
raised by subscriptions, endowments, annual collections, and school fees, "such as will enable a well
qualified schoolmaster to live in comfort and
respectability, if he devoted his whole time to the
duties of his vocation". It was doubtful whether
salaries raised from school fees would prove an
adequate remuneration for well-educated teachers,
and it was extremely precarious a livelihood which
relied on the charity of others. A teacher at
Ilkestone in 1841 was by trade a lace maker, and

60

when fully employed could earn £26 per year, whilst as a schoolmaster he earned £13. Most salaries ranged from £15 to £45 per year; and trained teachers from St. Mark's during the period 1841 to 1847 usually earned £50 to £90, although some earned as little as £18 and others as much as £130. It was common for teachers to be engaged in additional occupations, such as parish clerks and accountants, in order to increase their salaries.

1850-1870 The average salaries of certificated teachers in selected years during this period were as follows:

	Masters	Mistresses	Infant Mistresses
1855	£90/1/7	£60/11/5	£57/3/8
1859	£94/3/7	£62/13/10	£58/3/8
1865	£86/10/9	£55/2/1	£52/3/3
1868	£91/5/11	£56/1/7	£54/16/0

The decrease in the 1860s was the result of the Revised Code which removed the augmentation grants and introduced the system of payment by results. Thus, the livelihood of teachers was rendered more precarious than ever. Mistresses received less than masters, because, it was argued, they did not have family commitments, and the absence of government interest in the education of infants is reflected in the salaries of infant teachers. During the 1850s the salaries of masters were unlikely to fall below what they could earn as clerks, and those of mistresses contrasted favourably with other occupations; but the exodus from teaching in the 1860s suggests that this was no longer the case. The committee of a Liverpool school agreed in 1867 to compensate the master for the loss of salary which he had suffered since the Code was introduced. Certificated teachers whose salaries fell significantly below the average could earn as little as £30, less than was earned by drapers or other tradesmen. It was assumed that young men leaving college could earn salaries and emoluments of £70 or £80, and at the age of forty, this sum would have risen to £150. But there were numerous warehouses in Lancashire where with their education they could earn £50 to £100 per year for work far less arduous than the management of a village school.

1870-1901 After 1870 salaries rose, through the influence of school boards, particularly between 1870 and 1880, and this can be seen in the increases

61

which took place in average salaries. Those of
certificated masters rose by about 32% between
1870 and 1900, and those of certificated mistresses
by 46%. However, in 1890, 59.3%, and in 1900, 43.3%
of the certificated mistresses earned less than £75,
and if they had family responsibilities, their
standard of living was perilously close to Charles
Booth's definition of poverty. However, there were
very few other opportunities open to them, and they
could not therefore regard themselves as at a
disadvantage compared with other women who had been
similarly educated. The school boards were able to
pay higher salaries than the voluntary bodies, and
this situation persisted throughout the period. In
the 1890s teaching became attractive as a career to
many graduates who, in a reasonably short time could
anticipate promotion to headships in large schools;
but at the same time, managers of small voluntary
schools were replacing masters with mistresses at
lower salaries. After 1880 the percentage of schools
in England and Wales with accommodation for fewer
than sixty pupils was reduced, but in 1881 they were
31% of the total, and in 1891 they still accounted
for 22%. This situation was alleviated to some
extent in the grants which were made available
through the Voluntary Schools Act of 1897 which were
used for both additional appointments and higher
salaries.

In addition to their salaries, many teachers
received extra emoluments, which in the 1840s and
1850s included board and/or lodgings, a house and
garden, children's fees, candles, clothing, coal,
and food. In the Yorkshire District in 1855, 63%
of the certificated masters were provided with
either houses or lived rent free, but the other 37%
must have spent a considerable portion of their
income on accommodation. Large numbers of teachers
in National schools enjoyed housing facilities in
the 1870s, but these became more restricted as the
profession and school establishments grew. In 1878
46% of the masters and 34% of the mistresses were
provided with residences free of rent, but by 1900
the percentages which benefited were respectively
25 and 11.

Power was taken in the Minute of 1846 to grant
pensions and to facilitate the retirement of
superannuated certificated teachers, but this was
rescinded in 1862. A Select Committee of the House
of Commons in 1873 examined the possibility of

granting annuities to certificated teachers of public elementary schools upon their retirement due to age or ill-health. Some teachers had regarded the Minute of 1846 as a vested right to pensions, but this was denied by the Committee, which agreed however that 270 pensions of amounts ranging from £20 to £30 should be granted to certificated head teachers who were practising in 1862. Between 1875 and 1884 there were almost 1,000 applications for pensions in England, but only 572 were awarded; and even in 1895, only 691 were in receipt of pensions. The Cross Commission called for a superannuation scheme for teachers in 1888, a Departmental Committee reported 1895, and in 1898 an Act was passed for the provision of superannuation and other annuities and allowances to certificated teachers in elementary schools who had contributed to the scheme. The pensions were available to teachers on their retirement at sixty five years of age, or if certified mentally or physically unfit to continue in their vocation. Until the end of the century the majority of teachers could justifiably fear the prospect of sickness and old age, but in that their position did not differ from that of millions of working people in Britain.

An additional inducement to prospective teachers was the length of school holidays. During the period before 1870 they were chiefly related in country districts to the requirements of farmers. The schools were usually closed for at least four weeks at harvest, two at Christmas, and two at Easter, but frequently school work was suspended from the beginning of August until the end of November. This was of course a hardship to teachers who were deprived of school fees, and after 1862 were dependent on examination results for their remuneration. The gradual increase in holidays after 1870 may be seen in their provision by the Sheffield School Board, which in 1871 allowed for two weeks at Christmas, one week at Whitsuntide, two weeks at midsummer, one day on Easter Monday, and one half day on Shrove Tuesday. In 1875 the summer holiday was extended to three weeks(already the practice in voluntary schools), and Good Friday was included in the existing holidays. The position remained unchanged until 1892 when a fourth week was added to the summer holidays; the whole of Easter week was freed, but half day holidays were abolished.(44)

The Newcastle Commission reported in 1861 that

63

although the prospects of teachers were not as favourable as in some other professions, their employment was more secure.(45) The first Inspectors had been requested to enquire whether agreements between managers and teachers and facilities for dismissal existed. Teachers in voluntary schools were frequently extremely dependent on the local clergy, who as late as the 1890s could still apparently close schools arbitrarily if they were so inclined. James Runciman referred to the situation of many teachers in rural church schools who were subjected to "a galling tyranny, which they must endure unless they cared to risk social and professional ruin".(46) This was not calculated to attract competent men and women into teaching; but on the other hand, the growth of literacy would be obstructed if incompetent and unsuitable teachers benefited from a security of tenure. This was demonstrated in 1842 when the mistress of a girls' school in Liverpool was requested to resign after lady visitors had reported on the illiterate condition of the pupils.(47) The need to remove the large number of incompetent teachers which existed was realized at an early stage by the Committee of Council. It was possible for the certificates of teachers to be cancelled or temporarily suspended if they forged the registers, or were found guilty of drunkenness, embezzlement, and sexual immorality, and this power was exercised on a small number of occasions each year. The powers of the central authorities were not seemingly strong however as regards the dismissal of incompetent teachers, and the Cross Commission demanded, without success, that they should be strengthened by the suspension of grants to the schools concerned.

Whatever the limitations of salaries, pensions and emoluments, and security of tenure, teachers not only enjoyed a rising social prestige and long holidays, but could reasonably contrast their situation with that of their parents and acquaint-ances who were probably subject to intermittent unemployment and hardship. As in the influences on literacy which were cited in the first two chapters, much of the progress in the social and economic status and training of teachers during the 19th century took place between 1880 and 1900.

REFERENCES

1   Manchester Statistical Society, <u>Report on the state of education in the borough of Liverpool in 1835-1836</u>, p.vii.
2   State of Popular Education in England, <u>Report</u>(1861), Vol.3, p.516.
3   Ibid. Vol.1, pp.89, 95.
4   Robins, S., <u>Twenty reasons for accepting the Revised Educational Code</u>, p.17.
5   Committee of Council on Education, <u>Report</u>, 1865-1866, p.34.
6   Elementary Education Acts, <u>Final Report</u>(1888), p.81
7   Ibid. p.87.
8   Elementary schools(Dr. J. Crichton-Browne's Report)(1884), pp.34-9, 73.
9   Norris, J.P., <u>The education of the people</u>, p.18.
10   Elementary Education Acts, op. cit., p.93.
11   Kay, J., <u>The social condition and education of the people</u>, Vol.2, p.478.
12   Runciman, J., <u>Schools and scholars</u>,pp.134-9.
13   Select Committee on Education, <u>Minutes of evidence</u>(1835), pp.14-15.
14   State of Popular Education in England, op. cit., Vol.1, pp.52, 165-6.
15   Elementary Education Acts, op. cit., p.95.
16   Barnett, P.A., <u>Common sense in education</u>, pp.290-1.
17   Committee of Council on Education, op. cit., 1841-1842, p.189.
18   Anonymous, The educational crisis, <u>Quarterly Review</u>, 183(1896), p.58.
19   Spalding, T.A., <u>The work of the London School Board</u>, p.109.
20   Elementary Education Acts, op. cit., p.97.
21   Committee of Council on Education, op. cit., 1839-1840, p.82.
22   Anonymous, A visit to a training college, <u>Monthly Packet</u>, 14(1872), p.398.
23   Committee of Council on Education, op. cit., 1888-1889, p.443.
24   State of Popular Education in England, op. cit., Vol.1, pp.115, 116, 117, 119, 121-2, 123.
25   Royal Commission on Scientific Instruction, <u>Report</u>(1872), pp.xiii, xiv.
26   Huxley, T.H., <u>Science and education</u>, pp.170-71.
27   Committee of Council on Education, op. cit., 1854-1855, p.17.

28 Committee of Council on Education, op. cit.,
        1845, Vol.2, p.17.
29 Ibid. 1847-1848, Vol.2, p.481.
30 State of Popular Education in England, op. cit.
        Vol.1, pp.116, 130-1, 138.
31 Committee of Council on Education, op. cit.,
        1853-1854, Vol.1, pp.447-8.
32 Elementary Education Acts, op. cit., p.94.
33 Committee of Council on Education, op. cit.,
        1898-1899, p.317.
34 Runciman, J., op. cit., p.166.
35 Christian, G.A., English education from within,
        p.7.
36 Manchester Statistical Society, op. cit., p.19.
37 Buxton, S., Over-pressure, p.88.
38 Carter, T., Life and letters, p.32.
39 Kay, J., op. cit., Vol.2, p.483.
40 State of Popular Education in England, op. cit.
        Vol.1, p.163.
41 Anonymous, Our schools and schoolmasters,
        Quarterly Review, 146(1879), pp.175, 179.
42 Runciman, J., op. cit., pp.222, 267.
43 State of Popular Education in England, op. cit.
        Vol.1, p.162.
44 Bingham, J.H., The period of the Sheffield
        School Board, pp.88-91, 101.
45 State of Popular Education in England, op. cit.
        Vol.1, p.163.
46 Runciman, J., op. cit., pp.95-96.
47 Liverpool, Benevolent Society and Free School
        of St. Patrick, Committee book, August 1842.

4 School Buildings and Organization

he Committee of Council was concerned from its
nception that the education of children should not
e impeded by buildings unsuitable to their purpose.
n 1839 applicants for building grants were asked
o supply the Committee with information as to the
roposed sites; the provision for drainage; the
resence in the locality of tanneries, slaughter-
ouses, and other industries, and topographical
eatures potentially detrimental to health; together
ith structural details relating to walls, windows,
oofs, floors, heating, and ventilation. Particular
mphasis was to be given to the latter which was
of such importance to the health of the master and
he scholars, that it ought to be most carefully
onsidered". It is interesting to observe however
hat no mention was made of artificial lighting.
lans were made available so that new schools could
e built as efficiently as possible, and in a manner
hich had been proved to be most suitable.(1) The
fficial view of what constituted suitably construc-
ed schools changed in the light of increasing
xperience, and standards were raised, but the rules
f the Education Department for 1887 remained
xplicit that schools must be planned for both good
ealth and education. Particular attention was to be
iven to space requirements, adequate natural

lighting, and the provision of closets.

Throughout the period the voluntary bodies, concerned with the promotion of elementary educatic set standards of their own. In the 1830s the National Society estimated that seven square feet per child was a reasonable allocation of space, and regarded six square feet as a minimum provision. In the schools of the British and Foreign School Society the allocation of space per child was 7.7 square feet. Standards set by the Committee of Council fell from ten square feet in 1840 to six in 1845; after which they rose successively in 1856 to nine square feet, and in 1863 to ten square feet generally, and nine in larger schools. After 1870 however the Committee's requirement for grant aided schools was reduced to eight square feet per pupil as compared with a recommended ten square feet for the more affluent board schools. In practice this standard was not insisted upon, for in London board schools an allowance of ten square feet was not stipulated in graded schools until 1878, and in infant schools until 1899.(2) In view of this situation the Cross Commission would appear to have been in advance of current opinion in 1888 in recommending a minimum of ten square feet which it considered to more nearly represent "the indispensable requirements which have to be met",(3) but there was no consensus of opinion in this respect. It was not always possible to build schools large enough or in sufficient numbers to satisfy the requirements of localities owing to site limitation and sudden increases in population, and overcrowdin resulted.

Between 1839 and 1870 the unsatisfactory conditio of schools was reported by Inspectors with depressing regularity. Criticism was usually made of the inadequacy of accommodation, the sanitary defects, and heating, lighting, and ventilation. In the 1840 the school attached to St. Mark's, Whitechapel, consisted of "a portion of a house and two arches o Blackwall railway", and the Bermondsey ragged schoo was similarly situated twenty five years later.(4) In another instance the Inspector described a small room in which more than two dozen children sat on benches "in ranks closely packed".(5) Schools in the Midlands, Norfolk, and the North East were generally condemned by Inspectors for their lack of sanitation in the 1840s and 1850s; and many establishments in Lancashire were built "below the

evel of the earth" and were both damp and poorly
entilated. Complaints were made too of schools
ith high roofs beneath which the space became "a
ere reservoir of foul air" which constantly
escended into the room.(6)

  The schools which have been described were usually
nder inspection and were not considered to be by
ny means the worst available. Dame and private
chools, which are said to have represented almost
 0% of the total in the 1850s, were particularly
efective, and at the time of the Forster Act were
o be found in every town and in almost every
rillage in the land. The condition of these schools
as been widely described, and it is sufficient
herefore in the present instance merely to cite the
eport of one Inspector who visited

> a low room in a poor cottage, with no
> window that ever opens and a door that
> barely shuts, with a damp tiled floor
> and dingy walls, and seeming to reek
> with the exhalations of pent-up
> humanity.   (7)

n such a school

> the floor serves instead of benches;
> desks are not needed even if there were
> space for them...The closeness of the
> room makes animal heat save artificial
> fuel; and though foul air may for a time
> make the children restless, it soon acts
> as a narcotic.   (8)

  In contrast to the adverse reports which have been
cited, some Inspectors made favourable comments on
the buildings which they visited. Schools in London
in 1848 were with only two exceptions described as
'spacious and commodious...well lighted, lofty,
warmed and ventilated"; and in the West Country "for
the most part satisfactory, both in design and state
of repair".(9) Although it is possible to point to
conflicting statements, it is clear that the majority
of schools were in an unsatisfactory physical
condition. It was reasonable of course that a
proportion of the buildings should have been in good
condition as their construction was recent. Where
schools were even moderately suitable to their
purpose, they were still superior to the homes in
which large numbers of children lived.

  Significant improvements in school buildings were

made by school boards after 1870, although
initially they were often obliged to commence thei
activities in temporary premises. James Runciman
described an instance in which the London Board
"fitted up a long, hideous drill-room with rough
desks that served to seat 250 youngsters".(10) The
majority of voluntary schools which were transferr
to the Board in and after 1871 failed to reach the
standard which had been set for their continuance,
and were usually accepted only with a view to
replacement as soon as possible. T.A. Spalding, a
one time private secretary to the Chairman of the
London School Board, recorded several examples of
unsatisfactory schools which were transferred to
that body.(11)

Unfortunately the defects of the older schools
were not always avoided in the buildings which wer
constructed after 1870. The ceilings in many of th
newer schools were so high that the heating and
ventilation were rendered inadequate, and in
Sheffield in the 1890s, the board schools were so
draughty that Inspectors found it necessary to wea
their hats during inspection. Even when the
ventilation was adequate, teachers were frequently
careless in its use; and with regard to lighting,
it was complained that architects were more
interested in the appearance of ground glass window
than in the effect they were likely to have on the
sight of the children.(12) Inspectors' reports wer
frequently misleading in that a satisfactory review
of lighting during the summer could ignore the
defects of artificial lighting which became evident
during the winter; and schools which were comfortable during the winter were often fetid in the
summer months. It was suggested earlier that
artificial lighting was unsuitable for study for al
except the last decade of the century, and this was
relevant to schools as well as homes, particularly
as intellectual concentration was required in the
former, which need not obtain in the latter.
Although criticism continued to be made of the
heating, lighting, and ventilation of schools, very
little mention of sanitation was made in Inspectors
reports after 1870. On one occasion the Inspector
for the Northern Division referred to a "gradual
improvement in the sanitary condition of schools".(1
Complaints were sometimes made that in older
buildings the school room was also used as a cloak-
room, an unhealthy practice on wet days.

Voluntary schools were the subject of fairly frequent complaints in the closing decades of the century, and the Cross Commissioners drew attention to a "broad line of demarcation...between the accommodation provided by voluntary effort and that which has been created by school boards".(14) Many managers did not have access to sufficient money to improve the facilities of their schools and structural defects of various kinds were neglected. In 1891 an Inspector of schools in Lancashire commented that Preston and other districts where school boards had not been established should not be allowed to retain buildings which were inferior to those in comparable towns.(15) Inspectors were requested in 1892 and 1893 to report to the Committee of Council on the condition of school buildings in their areas, and in 1896 it was stated that with few exceptions their recommendations for improvement were implemented by managers of voluntary schools and by school boards. In the case of voluntary schools, large sums of money were raised, and the Committee was able to report that "a much higher and more satisfactory level has been reached both in regard to their fitness for educational work and their sanitary condition".(16)

Beneficial as they were to the physical condition of voluntary schools, government grants were not sufficient to ensure the maintenance of efficient standards. Between 1833 and 1853 the rate of grant was 2/6d.(12½p) per square foot if a teacher's house was included in the assessment, and in other cases, 1/8d.(8½p). In 1853 this was increased to 50% of the expense, but not in excess of 6/-(30p) per square foot, or 4/- if a school house was not included; but in 1859 the former was reduced to 4/- plus £100 for a house. The Minute of 1860 however stipulated that the grant must not exceed either the amount subscribed locally, or 2/6d. per square foot, or £65 for a house. Between 1839 and 1860, government grants for the construction, extension, and repair of elementary schools were approximately £1,000,000, but from 1860 to 1882 they were only £719,390. There were two reasons for this, namely the economies of the 1860s, and the refusal of the Committee of Council to entertain any further applications for building grants after 31st December 1870. The construction of new voluntary schools was carried out during the 1870s, and in 1882 the plans of 1870 were finally completed. After 1870, money for the

71

construction or extension of board schools was
borrowed from the Public Works Loan Commissioners,
rather than being obtained in the form of grants
from the Committee of Council on Education.

Having examined the state of school buildings and
the extent to which their construction was supported
by the Committee of Council, it is necessary to
discuss their adequacy for the children who were of
school age. Before 1870 it is almost impossible to
undertake a realistic analysis of the situation, as
no systematic assessment was made until 1871. In
1865 it was estimated that the average number of
pupils in attendance was probably only two thirds
of the total which could have been accommodated.
The Rev. J.P. Norris, for many years an Inspector
of Schools, claimed in 1869 that schools of varying
efficiency were available to all.(17) In contrast
to this however, it was reported in 1855 that new
schools were required in every part of London; and
in 1860 that large areas of the West Country were
without schools of any kind.(18) In rural areas
schools were not necessarily sited in the most
convenient positions. As prior to 1870 the
agricultural community constituted a large, if
decreasing, proportion of the population, the
gravity of this situation cannot be overlooked, and
the geographical difficulties were aggravated by
the unsystematic provision of schools by the
voluntary bodies.

After 1870 the accommodation provided in the
inspected schools of England and Wales was always
considerably in excess of the children in attendance

	Available Places	Average Daily Attendance
1875	3,146,424	1,837,180
1879	4,142,224	2,594,995
1886	5,145,292	3,438,425
1895	5,937,288	4,325,030
1900	6,544,092	4,687,646

The formula adopted in 1871 was the necessity to
make provision for 16% of the population, a
percentage which was restated in 1887.   Initially
the problem was to fill the schools which were
provided, and in some areas annual grants were
refused to schools which were considered surplus to
requirements; whilst in others, such as London in
1879, and Cromer and Norwich in 1888, there was
overcrowding.   The movement from the countryside
after 1870 resulted in surplus accommodation in

rural districts, but as has been seen, the growing towns were continually engaged in the construction and extension of schools. In order to provide efficient facilities in London, it was necessary to open a new school for one thousand children in each of ten months in every year.

An important factor in education was the manner in which schools were organized. Large unclassified groups of children are naturally at a disadvantage compared with those who are grouped by age and intelligence. Samuel Wilderspin, a leading advocate of infant education, emphasized this view, but in practice children were divided without reference to either.(19) For many years grouping tended to be by age, but by the 1880s a balance was increasingly struck between that and ability. J.G. Fitch recommended that children in a particular group should be of similar ability and attainment so that they could work together and stimulate intellectual development of each other.(20) The Code of 1884 stipulated that children must be classified with regard to "their health, their age, and their mental capacity, as well as their due progress in learning"; and the Code of 1890 aimed to give teachers freedom to group children in this way.

For examination purposes after 1862 the children were grouped into Standards. Until 1882 there were six Standards, but a seventh was introduced in that year. In the 1890s some school boards and voluntary bodies in England introduced an extra Standard, and others established the controversial "higher grade" elementary schools, in order to cater for the increasing numbers of children who were remaining at school for a longer period. A major disadvantage of the Standards system was the necessary arrange-ment of subjects for children of average ability, a factor which was detrimental to the education of brighter and duller children. In London board schools the brighter children were able to complete the work required of them in six months, and were then expected to cover the same ground for the remainder of the year. It could be claimed however that the majority of children attained the minimum educational standards which they could normally be expected to require in life. On the other hand, a witness before the Cross Commission calculated that in a given Standard, 20% of the children were undertaking work which was not sufficiently advanced for their abilities, and some 20 to 30% were attempting to cope with work beyond their abilities. The Cross Commission recommended that the Standards should be carefully revised, particularly in smaller schools, but claimed that they were too useful for examination purposes to be abolished.(21) A persistent abuse throughout the period was the presence in Standard I of three very different groups of children: those who could reasonably pass the examination, those who were slow learners, and those who were coerced into attendance and were almost entirely illiterate. If these groups of children were to benefit from their education, it was imperative that they should be separated. It is clear that the division of schools into Standards was educationally detrimental to a substantial minority of children, but it is difficult to envisage any other practical solution to the problem of insufficient teachers attempting to instruct large numbers of children in the early phase of the post-1870 period.

F.G. Gladman, who had wide experience as a training college principal, and an Inspector of Schools, pointed out that a well organized classification would result in children receiving the maximum benefit from all their lessons, and ideally every child should be placed in a class for each subject with other pupils of similar ability and attainment. The ideal was not generally implemented because for its realization it required a multiplicity of classrooms, an impossibility in the space which was normally available; and large numbers of teachers, which was also impossible unless expenditure was to be increased considerably. It was possible however to compromise by organizing a dual or tripartite classification in which basic groupings could be made according to ability in reading, writing, or arithmetic. This idea was not new, for in the early schools of the National Society, the children were sometimes classified according to reading ability, and in British schools by arithmetic and reading.(22)

In larger schools it was necessary to divide all except the highest Standards into classes, whilst in smaller schools all the children would sit in one room divided into Standards. In the 1830s and 1840s, schools which were organized according to the monitorial system were divided into classes of between eight and twelve children in British schools under the general supervision of the schoolmaster;

but where the system of simultaneous instruction was practised, as many as fifty children would be instructed in one class at one time. When the pupil-teacher system was introduced, the division of schools became more practicable, as pupil-teachers could usually be given more independence of action than monitors. Before the introduction of pupil-teachers, class rooms were available in many schools, but were frequently used for the storage of apparatus and lumber. One Inspector recommended in 1845 that work should be divided into three groups: subjects which required oral instruction by the head teacher, silent occupations such as writing and memorizing which were supervised by the pupil-teacher, and reading conducted by an assistant teacher and monitors. Each teacher concentrated on one or more subjects but did not develop any particular interest in the class.(23) As has been seen, the economies of the Revised Code in the 1860s, and the consequent temporary reduction in the numbers of pupil-teachers constituted a real threat to reasonably sized classes. Also a single system of classification became prevalent when the Code required that all children at a particular stage should be taught to a standard level.

The Committee of Council suggested in the 1840s that classes in schools should be separated by means of movable curtains which could be drawn back as necessary, but resulted in children still being distracted by activity in adjoining groups, almost as if no barriers existed. It was necessary for oral reading, for example, to be carried on not only where it would not distract other children, but where its progress could not be hindered by the work of others. Such activity could only be undertaken successfully in separate class rooms. Initially the large school room was regarded as the most important part of the building, and where class rooms were also provided, they were considered as accessories. Gradually the Prussian system of separate class rooms as the principal feature became popular in larger schools, and the big school room was increasingly used for assemblies. In 1871 the London School Board based its organization in elementary schools on the Prussian system, but modified it in order to avoid the number of teachers which would have been otherwise essential. In London schools, each pair of class rooms could be united by the use of screens and so make possible larger classes. The system in its entirety was more economical in Germany where teachers in the 1870s earned only 16% of the salaries commanded by their English colleagues.

Opinions varied as to the number of children who should be educated in one class. In 1839 it was considered necessary to divide a school of 160 children aged six to thirteen into four classes of forty pupils, and that the number of classes should be increased where there were more than 160. In 1871 the London and Sheffield School Boards attempted to make provision for classes of thirty, but in the former instance this plan was soon abandoned. Schools built later in the 1870s made provision for sixty children per class, an unwieldy number of pupils, and quite unsatisfactory for children in higher Standards. This situation was not improved until 1891 when the London Board began to provide at least two class rooms for higher Standards of not more than fifty children in selected schools. Not until 1900 however was the accommodation graduated to seat classes of not more than forty children in and above Standard VI, not more than fifty in Standards IV and V, and not more than sixty in Standards I to III. Whilst the London Board was regarded as progressive, its standards were lower than those considered adequate by the Cross Commissioners, who called for a maximum of forty children per class in all except the highest Standards, and twenty five in the latter. In the 1890s the classes in some board schools consisted of between seventy and one hundred pupils. In practice the subjects to be taught largely influenced the sizes of classes. Oral teaching was effective with large groups, and it was possible to combine two or even more classes for this purpose. In contrast, reading which requires a considerable amount of individual practice, was more appropriately taught in small groups selected from a class so that the teacher could more easily ascertain the progress of each child.

Well organized infant schools were instrumental in inculcating the mechanics of reading into young children. Samuel Wilderspin claimed that the first "systematized school" was established in 1820,(24) and many schools were opened, particularly between 1830 and 1835, through the influence of Lord Brougham and the Marquess of Lansdowne, who were respectively Lord Chancellor and Lord President of the Council in those years. In 1835 there were approximately 2,000 infant schools of varying efficiency which accommodated 64,000 pupils. The term "infant school" however, was subjected to a liberal interpretation, for example the infant schools in Liverpool at the time were mainly connected with public elementary schools, and were little more than nurseries. The Newcastle Commission sought to differentiate between these and schools which were well organized, and in which the children were able to read and write by the age of seven. After 1867 there was no competition from agriculture and industry for the services of children under seven, and there can be no doubt that the infant school provided the only education which many children were likely to receive. A child who had been taught in an infant school, and proceeded to an elementary school at seven, could make as much progress by the age of ten as another child not similarly educated would make by the age of twelve. Increasingly the demand was made for separate classes, or in larger schools, departments; but a survey of 184,000 pupils in ten districts in 1858 revealed that only 14% were taught in separate infant schools in spite of the fact that over 30% were aged between three and seven. Obstacles to the growth of infant schools included the expense involved in accommodation and special teachers; and in country districts where the population was scattered, it was unreasonable to expect young children to walk long distances to inconveniently situated schools. Where schools were established, they were often expected to cater for children who were too young to benefit from formal education, and frequently, the infant class mainly consisted of pupils not sufficiently advanced for promotion to Standard I. There was too, a lack of continuity between infant schools and the first Standard, and the children were required to repeat in the latter the lessons learned in the former. The Committee of Council was concerned with economy, and the Code of 1884 stated that a separate infant class could not be formed when the average attendance was less than twenty. In the Code of 1885 it was emphasized that the younger children who for lack of numbers could not constitute a separate class, should still receive instruction suitable to their age. In the 1870s and 1880s the provision of infant schools became more widespread; and the problem of numbers was largely resolved when the deterring fees

were abolished in 1891, and younger children were
increasingly sent to school. Infant education had
always been important even if this was not always
recognized, but in terms of numbers, it became
essential after 1891.

Towards the end of the 19th century, larger
schools were divided into a number of departments.
In London the departments in particular schools
could include the boys', girls', senior mixed, and
junior mixed, as well as infants'. The maximum
accommodation in one complex was not intended to
exceed places for 1,548 children, divided equally
into boys' and girls', and infants' departments;
and if additional accommodation was required it was
provided by a separate mixed department.(25) In
English education the concept of mixed schools, with
the exception of infants' schools, was almost always
viewed in terms of economic expediency rather than
academic advantage. Wesleyan schools were notable
exceptions to the general attitude, and in them
co-education was frequently encountered. An interest
in the needs of individual children cannot be easily
identified, except in isolated instances. The
division of larger schools into departments
according to the sex of children surely conflicts
with the awareness of classification by ability and
attainment, and the policy in London strengthens
the conclusion that organizational techniques were
confused. On the other hand, Victorian educators
were also aware of the lack of moral sense said to
prevail among large sections of the lower classes
throughout the period, a factor which was likely to
take precedence over educational theories.

The length of the school day had a direct
influence on the academic performance of children.
For much of the Victorian period the school day
consisted of six hours, and intervals between
lessons were uncommon. In British schools in 1861
the hours of school were from 9.0 a.m. to 12 noon,
and from 2.0 p.m. to 5.0 p.m., and it was considered
doubtful whether this was satisfactory. A
contributor to The Quarterly Review suggested that
a school day of three or four hours was sufficient
for most children, although he was a supporter of
the half-time system, the advantages of which have
been discussed.(26) Nassau Senior quoted the

78

opinions of a number of teachers who considered that
a four hour day was adequate if it was divided into
two hours and a half in the morning and one hour and
a half in the afternoon. One teacher advocated a
school day of three hours for infants, three hours
and a half for children aged seven to ten, and four
hours for children aged ten to thirteen.(27) The
normal school hours in the 1880s were less by one
half hour than those which obtained twenty years
earlier, a length of time which was regarded by Dr.
Crichton-Browne as adequate, and which of course
was similar to practice in the latter decades of
the twentieth century. However, at examination
times large numbers of children were detained in
school after the normal hours, often for long
periods.(28) It was reasonable to suggest that the
length of the school day should depend partly on
the character of school work and partly on the
physical condition of the building.(29) The
situation could be eased if the timetable was
planned so that perhaps a total of four hours were
devoted to intellectual pursuits, two to manual
activities, an additional period to homework, and
intervals provided during the day for rest and
recreation. The length of lessons was also
important if children were to remain attentive, and
David Donaldson of the Glasgow Free Church College
advocated the following periods in 1861:

> Children aged five to seven   Fifteen minutes
> Children aged seven to ten   Twenty minutes
> Children aged ten to twelve   Thirty minutes (30)

A particular difficulty was encountered among the
many children who were coerced into school
attendance after 1870, for they were often
incapable of sustained thought, and it was
impossible to interest them in any subject for more
than five minutes at a time.(31) In the Revised
Instructions to Inspectors which related to the Code
of 1891 the Committee of Council was reasonably
specific as regards the length of time for lessons
in infant schools:

> It is essential...that the length of the
> lesson should not...exceed thirty minutes,
> and should be confined in most cases to
> twenty minutes; and that the lessons
> should be varied in length according to
> the section of the school, so that in the
> babies' room the actual work of the

lesson should not be more than a quarter
of an hour. Each lesson should be followed
by intervals of rest and song.

The ventilation of schools was often inadequate,
and in such circumstances, it was necessary that
children should not remain in rooms for longer than
one hour at a time if they were not to become
listless. One critic of the existing situation went
so far as to suggest that "to work continuously in
a close stuffy room is slow suicide";(32) and it
was important that at the end of each hour the
class or school room should be ventilated.

The concept of homework was supported in the years
prior to 1860 as a means to improved results, and
in 1884 the Committee of Council expressed approval
of the practice except in the cases of delicate or
very young children. Unfortunately the living
conditions of many children were not conducive to
intellectual activities, and as has been seen, the
unsuitable lighting which existed was harmful to
their sight, with the predictable consequence that
home work was often neglected. Teachers in London
opposed the practice, but it was pointed out that
if home lessons were abolished, it would be
necessary to increase the amount of work undertaken
during the day, in order to meet the requirements
of the Code. The Committee of Council regarded the
imposition of home work as the responsibility of
individual head teachers, but in the light of Dr.
Crichton-Browne's report, it was decided in 1884
that the practice must not be obligatory. However,
after the report had been made, Crichton-Browne is
said to have informed J.G. Fitch that "there was
much less to complain of than he expected to find
in the use of home lessons in the elementary schools
of London".(33)

The education of backward, mentally defective,
blind, deaf and dumb children was generally
neglected with the exception of work undertaken by
voluntary organizations. In varying degrees all
these defects impeded the growth of literacy in the
children concerned, but it was impossible to cater
for the individual needs of backward children, for
example, in the often insufficiently staffed country
schools which contained children of a wide range of

ntelligence. Slow learners were a source of
rritation to normal children when they were placed
n ordinary classes, and frequently the work of
nfant schools was undermined by their presence.
'he problem was aggravated after 1870 when
ompulsory education was introduced. The necessity
'or children in and above Standard I to pass in a
ligher Standard each year constituted a hardship for
he 20% or 30% who were expected to undertake work
eyond their ability, and there were complaints of
undue pressure being placed on these children. It
vas of course possible after 1884 for children to
e presented on more than one occasion in the same
Standard in exceptional circumstances. A suggested
advantage of the Revised Code was that teachers
eager to qualify for higher grants were not tempted
o ignore backward children. Also, although the
ndividual examination of children in infant schools
vas discontinued after 1870, it was maintained in
he case of children in these schools who were over
seven years of age. A basic problem was that
nsufficient was known of the causes and extent of
ackwardness among children in English elementary
schools, and Dr. Crichton-Browne showed perception
n dividing children into three categories: the
lull, the starved, and the delicate.(34) Not until
1896 was a Committee appointed to enquire into the
existing educational provision for backward
children, and the need was shown for discrimination
etween the educable and the ineducable. In 1898
the Committee recommended the establishment of
reparatory classes in separate rooms for which in
smaller schools the infant mistress would be
esponsible, and in larger schools a special teacher
appointed.

A distinction was not drawn between mentally
defective children and slow learners, although some
of the former have been known in time to understand
the basic mechanics of reading. In 1895 it was
estimated that there were 80,000 mentally defective
children in England and Wales;and in order that
their needs might be met, a permissive Education
(Defective and Epileptic Children)Act was passed in
1899. This empowered school boards to provide
special accommodation for defective children, either
in public elementary schools or specially certified
schools; and it stipulated that the children
concerned should be educated until they were
sixteen years of age. Two special schools had been

opened for mentally defective children in London in 1892, but by 1900 the Board controlled fifty three centres in which children were taught scripture, reading, writing, arithmetic, and other subjects.

Throughout the 19th century provision was made for blind children by voluntary organizations, and by 1870 schools were available in the majority of larger conurbations, the earliest having been founded at Liverpool in 1791. The schools aimed to render the pupils as independent as possible and as literate as was necessary, with the assistance of books which were either in braille or contained letters of the traditional alphabet in relief. The Poor Law authority was the only public body in the country with powers to educate blind children, but there was a reluctance to request its assistance. Between 1870 and 1890 some school boards such as those at Bradford and London established schools for the blind, and together with the voluntary organizations, succeeded in placing under instruction a large number of blind children. In London, a peripatetic teacher was appointed by the Board in 1875 to instruct blind children in ordinary schools, and centres were established four years later. Conferences were held in London and Manchester in 1889 which resolved that the education of blind children should be made subject to the Education Acts and Codes of Instruction either in Day schools, independent institutions, or establishments provided by groups of education authorities; and in the same year the Royal Commission on the Blind, Deaf and Dumb, etc., recommended that not only should the education of these children be placed under government inspection, but also the age of compulsory instruction should be extended in their case to sixteen years. The obligatory Elementary Education(Blind and Deaf Children)Act of 1893 empowered school boards to provide for the education of blind and deaf children, and without exception the age of compulsory attendance was fixed at sixteen years. By 1898 there were twenty two certified residential institutions and sixteen Day schools in England, at which blind children were educated; facilities which were quite inadequate, particularly in rural areas, but nationally, no part of the country was remote from a centre for the education of blind children. Although normal certificated teachers without special training were able to teach blind children f they learned the system of reading and writing, pecially qualified teachers were appointed, and in ach school the head or deputy was usually required o be blind.

Partially sighted children were at a disadvantage n reading as it was difficult for them to focus rint clearly, and even mild degrees of muscular nbalance could result in eyestrain if neglected. arge numbers of children suffered from ocular efects, and although spectacles were sometimes rovided by school boards, as at Sheffield from 885, comparatively few pupils used the service. In eneral, little attention was specially given to hildren with ocular defects, although in 1897, irculars were distributed to heads of Sheffield oard schools which requested that the sight of upils be tested and parents asked to have defects orrected. Similar treatment was introduced at radford a year later. Eye complaints were of course ggravated where school lighting was poor.

In the early years of the 19th century, deaf mutes ere commonly regarded as mentally defective; and he opening of a school in Liverpool in 1825 was rogressive indeed in making it possible for hildren who lived at home to be taught reading, riting, arithmetic, and other subjects. By 1861, he attitude to the deaf had changed, and of 12,000 ho were so afflicted in England and Wales, it was stimated that approximately 2,000 would benefit rom education, twice as many as were at that time nder instruction. Ten years later there were nstitutions in several large towns in which the ajority of pupils were aged seven and eight; and chools were opened by the London and Sheffield oards in 1874 and 1878. The education of deaf and umb children was, as has been seen, considered by he Royal Commission of 1889, and legislative rovision was made in the Act of 1893. The problem as that parents were often reluctant to admit that heir children were deaf, but in spite of this, by 895 the schools were being widely used. The ecruitment of suitable staff was a problem which as not easily resolved, with the result that there as no provision whatever for deaf children in East nglia and parts of the Home Counties. Provision as possible in many areas only where groups of chool boards co-operated, and an outstanding xample of this was demonstrated in North Stafford-hire. It was not the practice however to test the hearing of children before the 20th century, and the danger of deafness did not appear to be sufficiently appreciated by the authorities.

The legislation of the 1890s respecting mentally and physically handicapped children was of little or no benefit to children at school in the last decade of the century. Had it not been for the spasmodic and isolated activity of voluntary bodies and individuals, the education of these children would have been non-existent.

REFERENCES

1   Committee of Council on Education, <u>Report</u>,
    1839-1840, pp.5-7, 11, 26, 46, 56-92, 126-172.
2   Spalding, T.A., <u>The work of the London School
    Board</u>, p.68
3   Elementary Education Acts, <u>Final Report</u>(1888),
    p.64.
4   Committee of Council on Education, op. cit.,
    1844, Vol.2, p.116; 1872-1873, p.169.
5   Ibid. 1844, Vol.2, p.9.
6   Ibid. 1855-1856, p.354; 1859-1860, p.58.
7   Ibid. 1872-1873, p.94.
8   State of Popular Education in England, <u>Report</u>
    (1861), Vol.3, pp.481-2.
9   Committee of Council on Education, op. cit.,
    1847-1848, Vol.1, p.55; Vol.2, p.78.
10 Runciman, J., <u>Schools and scholars</u>, p.4.
11 Spalding, T.A., op. cit., pp.54-5, 59-60.
12 Bingham, J.H., <u>The period of the Sheffield
    School Board</u>, p.50.
13 Committee of Council on Education, op. cit.,
    1886-1887, pp.264-5.
14 Elementary Education Acts, op. cit., p.62.
15 Committee of Council on Education, op. cit.,
    1891-1892, p.349.
16 Ibid. 1895-1896, p.iv.
17 Norris, J.P., <u>The education of the people</u>, p.17.
18 Committee of Council on Education, op. cit.,
    1855-1856, pp.215-6; 1859-1860, p.54.
19 Select Committee on Education, <u>Minutes of
    Evidence</u>(1835), pp.14-15.
20 Fitch, J.G., <u>Lectures on teaching</u>, p.59.
21 Elementary Education Acts, op. cit., pp.134,135.
22 Gladman, F.J., <u>School work</u>, pp.15, 18, 36-7,
    39, 40.
23 Committee of Council on Education, op. cit.,
    1847-1848, Vol.2, pp.4, 127.
24 Select Committee on Education, op. cit., p.13.
25 Bailey, T.J., The planning and construction of
    board schools, <u>Royal Institute of British
    Architects Journal</u>, 6(1899), pp.407-8.
26 Anonymous, Education of the poor, <u>Quarterly
    Review</u>, 110(1861), pp.510-511.
27 Senior, N.W., <u>Suggestions in popular education</u>,
    pp.243-75.
28 Elementary Schools(Dr. J. Crichton-Browne's
    Report(1884), p.5.
29 Currie, J., <u>The principles and practice of</u>

      <u>common school education</u>, p.150.

30 Senior, N.W., op. cit., p.274.
31 Runciman, J., op. cit., p.7.
32 Landon, J., op. cit., p.177.
33 Elementary Schools(Dr. J. Crichton-Browne's
      Report)(1884), pp.5, 31, 68.
34 Ibid. pp.4, 5, 7.

5 Teaching Methods and the Curriculum

The first Inspectors enquired into the methods of instruction in schools, and judging by the questions they were requested to ask, it would appear that the Committee of Council assumed that teachers adhered to the systems either of mutual or simultaneous instruction, The system of mutual instruction, or the monitorial system, was discredited by Inspectors in the 1840s, but most teachers were ignorant of any other approach, and it lingered until at least 1860. The advantage of simultaneous instruction was the supervision at all times by the teacher and not by monitors. In small schools the system of simultaneous instruction was practised in and after the 1830s, and it became more popular in larger schools after the introduction of pupil-teachers in 1846.

Most teachers in the 1840s did not possess the technical expertise to act independently, but the influence of training colleges was to ensure that even if experiments in method were not undertaken, subjects would be taught with greater efficiency. For many years teachers appeared to be solely concerned with the subject matter of instruction, and each class learned the same lessons by rote as if the children were intellectually identical. Not until after 1870 was there significant evidence that the individuality of pupils was reflected in

87

the methods which were used. J.G. Fitch claimed
in 1880 that "it may well be doubted whether at the
present stage of our educational experience any bod
of rules whatever could be safely formulated and
declared the best". He considered that teachers
should be given the opportunity to adapt methods to
their own special circumstances and requirements.(1
In the 1890s more freedom was in fact given to
teachers to develop methods which were both suitabl
to their abilities and of benefit to the children.
It was increasingly recognized that one of the
primary objects of education was to encourage
children to acquire knowledge for themselves and no
to be expected to listen for long periods to a
teacher. By the end of the century it was beginning
to be accepted that not only must children be
treated as individuals in the process of developmen
but also that they differ mentally, physically, and
in their experience. It was also true however, that
the education of individuals must take place in
groups of children of similar ability and attainment. In the light of later experiments in the non-
streaming of children and the organization of
classes into mixed ability and family groupings,
this idea has of course been criticized.

It is almost impossible to decide the most
efficient method of teaching reading for three
principal reasons: it tends to be determined by
fashion, it is difficult to define precisely what
each method includes, and it is impossible to asses
the skill of teachers who adopt each method. The
contrasting of modern with Victorian methods is not
therefore necessarily valuable, inasmuch as the
former will probably be condemned and superseded in
their turn as has so often occurred in the past.

Then as now it was accepted that reading may be
learned in two ways, by analysis and by synthesis.
The most popular method in the 19th century was the
alphabetic, which is synthetic in character. It
consisted of teaching children the forms of letters
attaching to the forms certain arbitrary names, and
then combining the forms and names into words which
had little or no resemblance in sound to the names
by which the individual forms had been designated.
The children were taught to say "em - wi" is "my"
and "aitch - o - yew - ess - ee" is "house". It was
appreciated that the letters of the alphabet bore
no relationship to the sounds of words, but
exponents of the method claimed that it helped to

concentrate the attention of pupils on the various parts of words. Critics quite reasonably complained that it was unsatisfactory for children to spell out single words without any regard to sense; and in the 1840s J.P. Kay-Shuttleworth, at that time secretary of the Committee of Council on Education, advocated the use of the phonic method. In support of the phonics the Committee criticized teachers for restricting themselves to a "purely dogmatic method of instruction in reading, exercising no faculty but that of memory".(2) The phonic method was not universally applauded by any means, and was subjected to scathing criticism by an anonymous writer in The Quarterly Review, who concluded that "no child who shall be treated exclusively after Dr. Kay-Shuttleworth's method, and limited to his reading lessons, will ever be able to read at all".(3) Gradually however criticism of the method diminished and the teaching of reading by phonics was increasingly recommended by educationists. According to this method children had first to recognize the elements of sounds and were then shown how the sounds could be combined to form words. Each child progressed from simpler to more difficult sounds and combinations, and was able therefore to cultivate his reasoning faculties in word building. S.S. Laurie, for many years secretary and visitor of schools to the education committee of the Church of Scotland, claimed that a child who learned to read alphabetically obtained no assistance from letters until he had "unconsciously and gradually worked out for himself a complete phonic system".(4)

The principal objection to the teaching of reading by the phonic method to English children is that English is not a phonetic language, but Laurie dismissed this criticism as trivial and made the astonishing statement that

> "be - a - te" does not, when rapidly pronounced, yield precisely "bat"... but it very nearly yields it, especially if an effort is made to sink the vowel element in the sound, and in a great number of words it quite yields it. (5)

It has often been claimed that children taught by the phonic method are apt to become so absorbed in the mechanical task of sounding the separate phonemes in an unfamiliar passage that little energy remains for intelligent reading. The concentration on phonics

may also be condemned for the limited and
uninteresting vocabulary which it was thought
necessary to use, such as:

    My dog is in the bog
    My hog is in the bog
    My cat is in the bog
    My rat is in the bog
    My pig is in the bog, etc   (6)

The analytic approach was exemplified in the "look
and say" or word method, in which words were learned
by sight and later analysed into their components.
The method had originated in the work of Comenius,
and was advocated by exponents in the 19th century
because it appeared to offer more interest to the
pupil as the words used were drawn from his existing
vocabulary, and not subordinated to the artificial
requirements of phonics. John Gill of Cheltenham
Training College was one who appeared to favour the
"look and say" method, although he admitted that it
is defective in that it cultivates the memory rather
than the reason, and cannot effectively encourage
word building.(7)

Although each method had its devotees, the virtue
of a systematic combination of systems was recognized throughout the Victorian period, the tendency
being to commence with phonics, continue with "look
and say", and then to combine the two. It is
probable that as educationists were preoccupied with
the need to replace the alphabetic method with the
phonic, they regarded the "look and say" method as
supplementary to the teaching of reading, and did not
recognize in it a potent means of arousing the
initial interest of children, who are likely to
memorize words with greater facility than they can
rationalize, at least in the initial stages.

Dr. James Currie, Principal of the Church of
Scotland Training College in Edinburgh,drew
attention in 1862 to a method for teaching reading
in which temporary use could be made of an augmented
roman alphabet in which the characters were
sufficiently numerous to represent all the phonemes
of the English language. A transition could later be
made to the traditional alphabet and continuity be
ensured by the use of the same primers in which only
the alphabet was changed.(8) Augmentations of the
English alphabet had been devised from the 16th
century, but it is possible that Currie was
describing the particular system known as Phonotypy

which had been developed in the 1840s by Isaac
Pitman and Alexander Ellis. Phonotypy was used in
numerous experiments, chiefly in schools in the
United States, but in some instances in Britain,
although it did not attract widespread support until
its introduction as the initial teaching alphabet
more than a century later. A contributor to Punch
in 1848 commented that "madness had adopted a
variety of methods, and run the round of almost
every absurdity; but decidedly the most insane thing
out of Bedlam in the present day, is a scheme for...
the utter or unutterable confusion of all
orthography".(9)   James Spedding, chiefly known for
his editorship of the works of Bacon, claimed that
children who began with Pitman's alphabet were able
to read and spell in the conventional orthography
more quickly than those who did not.(10)

At the end of the century, Nellie Dale introduced
an approach to reading in which initially only
regular words were used, and all which presented
difficulties were excluded. Her more radical
innovation was the use of colour to indicate the
broad distinctions between vowels, voiced consonants,
voiceless consonants, and silent letters. In the
preface to Miss Dale's book on the teaching of
reading, her head mistress wrote that this aid to
teaching had turned "the arid tearful desert of the
spelling and reading lesson into the most enchanting
of fairy gardens". Miss Dale claimed that the use
of different colours gave pleasure to the children
who found no difficulty in transferring to texts
printed in black.(11) However, problems were likely
to arise where children were colour blind, a defect
which afflicts about 4% of the male population.
Nellie Dale's influence was minimal in the 19th
century, but the use of colour was to be more widely
adopted of course through the work of Dr. Caleb
Gattegno after 1960.

It has been shown that some importance was
attached to arousing the interest of children in
reading. Variety of subject matter was thought to
be necessary as children had wide interests, but it
was also essential to relate content and vocabulary
to the comprehension and experience of children.
This could be ensured in the content of reading
books, but a common method of arousing interest in
reading was to show children objects. One writer
was explicit that, in the initial stages, reading
lessons from books were designed to enable children

to recognize in print words with which they were familiar, but the extension of vocabulary was best undertaken in "object and other conversational lessons".(12) It was argued that if children encountered in books the terms they had learned from objects, they would recognize them immediately, and in many instances objects were used in preference to books. The tedium of reading lessons was likely to be reduced if as much factual information as possible was imparted. It became recognized however, that initially, "attention should be concentrated on the act of learning to read, without endeavouring to extend the bounds of the pupil's knowledge".(13) The solution was to use familiar topics, and only at a later stage to regard the book as a vehicle for information. The practice of using objects was still in vogue at the end of the century, and was appreciated by children, who not only provided specimens, but also suggested topics for future talks. From 1884 the Instructions to Inspectors made specific reference to the merits of object lessons in the teaching of reading. The use of suitable objects in reading lessons for older children was advocated in the Revised Instructions to Inspectors in 1896. In addition to objects, Nellie Dale had advocated the use of pictures, songs, poetry, modelling, and painting, as aids to the teaching of reading.(14)

A constant problem in the teaching of reading was that even where children learned to read fluently, they seldom did so with intelligence. This defect could reasonably be traced not only to the mechanical character of the alphabetic and phonic methods of teaching reading, but also to the unreasoning memorization necessitated by the "look and say" method. Toward the end of the century more appropriate methods were adopted, as trained teachers were allowed greater independence of action in their work; and it was gradually seen to be important that teachers should employ any method which suited the needs of individual children. An obstacle to this development was the general practice in schools of whole classes reading by rote, and individual progress being ignored or neglected. One aspect of the problem was the variance which existed between standard English and the vernacular of working class children, so that the reading lesson frequently presented difficulties normally encountered in the learning of a foreign language. It is natural that the standards of the community were more influential than those of the school, and the linguistic habits inculcated during the limited time at the disposal of the latter were constantly undermined by the former. There could be no doubt that the elementary school had to "fight against the low standard of the home in language as in other things".(15)

As the opinion spread in educational circles that children must be treated as individuals, there was considerable discussion as to the most opportune time for them to learn to read. At least one critic thought that a commencement should not be made until a child was at least four years of age. In the 1890s John Dewey and other American educationists, insisted that early attention to reading was detrimental to children, and it should not be introduced until the age of eight. A contrasting view was that if children were not taught to read between five and eight, they would not be interested in learning to read.

The Revised Code of 1862 exerted a theoretically beneficial but practically pernicious influence on the growth of literacy. Until the Code the government did not exercise direct control over the curriculum. Whilst in 1851 most schools were concerned only with reading, writing, and arithmetic, some teachers introduced a variety of subjects such as etymology, geography, grammar, history, and science. This was criticized by the Rev. Sanderson Robins, who stated his belief that additional subjects were wasted on "the village lad whose outdoor life begins almost before his childhood ends". He considered that "we shall not render the child of the farm servant a real benefit if we substitute a superficial knowledge of two or three such subjects at the expense of the preliminary instruction which furnishes the key to all. We must not allow the pretence of learning more to produce...the result of knowing less".(16) Nassau Senior, on the other hand, complained not of the number of subjects which were taught, but of the tendency to inculcate vast quantities of factual information.(17) It was the proven failure to teach successfully either the three basic or the additional subjects which induced the Newcastle Commission to recommend a system of payment on the basis of examination results in reading, writing, and arithmetic, and this was effected in the Revised Code. This resulted in a discontinuation in all but a

small minority of instances of the teaching of other
unremunerative subjects. Supporters of the Code of
1862 claimed that teachers were aware of the
examination requirements and could prepare pupils
accordingly; there was to be a measure of standard-
ization in all schools and a stipulated level of
progress was to be ensured. They suggested that
children would receive a solid foundation in the
elementary subjects which would equip them for their
anticipated role in life. Robins considered that the
failure in education prior to 1862 was the result of
a "want of industry, conscientiousness, and the
sense of duty" in the teaching profession.(18) In
theory the Revised Code ought to have resulted in
a greater efficiency in teaching, but in practice a
significant rise in the level of literacy was not
realized, and in 1868 the results in the reading
examination were only 2% higher than in 1864. John
Morley wrote that in one school he heard every
child in Standard I read without difficulty from his
set book, but none was able to read the most simple
words in a similar but hitherto unseen volume.(19)
Similar complaints were made in Inspectors reports,
that teachers concentrated on drilling children in
the rudiments because intellectual instruction was
not remunerative, and repetition was a certain means
to high grants. Fortunately the Code was gradually
liberalized(see Appendix 1)so that from 1868 grants
were extended to one extra subject in addition to
reading, writing, and arithmetic, and from 1871 more
subjects were added including English literature.
The emphasis on examinations was reduced so that
from 1890 only a selection of children were examined;
and from 1895 the examination was replaced by simple
inspection. The principal contribution of these
amendments in terms of literacy was the opportunity
to extend the linguistic experience of children
through the great works of literature, and to
transfer the emphasis from repetition to comprehension in reading.

It is of interest to investigate the standard of
literacy which remained low during the decade
following the distribution to the religious
societies of the first Parliamentary Grant of 1833.
The situation in the North West was perhaps typical
of the national level, in that whilst many working
class children in attendance at school read with
fluency, very few did so with intelligence. In 1842

the endowed school at Yaxley in Huntingdonshire
consisted of fifteen boys aged between five and
eleven, of whom three could read a simple verse from
the New Testament, eight could read easy words with
varying degrees of accuracy, and four could identify
only letters. A report from the Midlands in 1844
revealed that of 11,782 children in attendance at
elementary schools, less than half could read
letters and monosyllables; a third, easy narratives
but not including the Bible; and 17%, the Bible. In
the British schools of 1846, only 10% of the boys
read with ease and less than 1% with intelligence.
The girls were more proficient, 80% reading with
ease and 5% with apparent understanding. These
standards were comparable with those which generally
obtained in National schools. The Rev. Henry Moseley,
H.M.I., reported in 1847 on the district comprising
Berkshire, Hampshire, and Wiltshire, in which he
revealed that a slightly larger proportion of
children could read in the south of England. He
claimed that of a school population of 6,213, 17%
could read the Bible fluently, 50% simple passages
from the Gospels, and 33% letters and monosyllables.
The percentage of children in Middlesex who could
read letters and monosyllables but not simple
narratives, fell from 40% in 1850 to 28% in 1853,
but there was in fact real progress, as the apparent
deterioration resulted from the inclusion from 1851
of statistics relating to infants. The reading of
younger children required, but did not receive,
special attention. Standards of reading showed some
improvement in the church schools of Cheshire and
the North Midlands between 1859 and 1861; and whilst
in the former year it was estimated that 25% of the
children could read a familiar primer, the proportion in the latter year had risen to one third. On
the other hand, only 8% could read whatever was
placed before them.(20)

At this point it is intended to ascertain what
academic performance was required of and obtained
from children in their reading. It was considered
reasonable in 1835 that children of seven years of
age who had attended an infant school should be able
to read any book written in "simple language";(21)
and in 1862 Dr. Currie wrote that such children
ought to read fluently "easy narratives and the
simpler parts of the Bible".(22) In 1875 however,
an Inspector estimated the anticipated performance
of infants as follows:

Age

4 - 5   To name or point out the letters in
         an alphabet card.
5 - 6   To read words of three letters, about
         eight pages.
6 - 7   To read words of one syllable, about
         thirty additional pages.

He claimed that in his district the average pass in
reading in 1875 was 79% in the first group, 73% in
the second, and 75% in the third.(23) Thus the
standards appear to have been too high for between
20% to 30% of the children who would certainly have
found difficulty in attaining the level set by Dr.
Currie. It would be difficult also to obtain books,
apart from specially written primers, or Biblical
passages confined to words of one syllable.

Before 1862 standards of attainment in elementary
schools were not stipulated, but in that year the
standards of reading imposed by the Revised Code
were assumed to be those which working class
children would need for their "business in life":(24)

Standard

I   Narrative in monosyllables.

II   One of the narratives next in order
       after monosyllables in an elementary
       reading book used in the school,

III   A short paragraph from an elementary
       reading book used in the school.

IV   A short paragraph from a more
       advanced reading book used in the
       school.

V   A few lines of poetry from a reading
       book used in the first class of the
       school.

VI   A short ordinary paragraph in a
       newspaper, or other modern
       narrative.

The vagueness of such terms as "a few lines" and "a
short paragraph" were surely subject to varying
interpretation, and conflicted with the intention to
standardize educational requirements. The inherent
defect of newspapers and other contemporary
narratives in reading lessons was that they had been
written primarily to inform, but not to instruct
children. Fowler's The King's English demonstrates
this clearly, not only in the misuse of language by

uch authors as Charlotte Brontë, Charles Dickens,
and George Eliot, but also in the columns of The
Times newspaper. However, difficulties of this kind
could easily be overcome if teachers drew attention
to the errors. In each case the language could be
fully criticized, and where necessary corrected,(25)
a situation which was of course dependent upon the
pupil/teacher ratio in each class.

In the Code of 1871 the six Standards were
modified and a higher level of attainment required.
Standard I was abolished, the other five renumbered,
and a new Standard VI added, in which children were
expected "to read with fluency and expression".
Minor changes were introduced in the Codes between
1873 and 1880: emphasis was placed in 1875 on
intelligent reading in all except Standard I, and
the recitation of poetry was demanded in Standards
IV, V, and VI. The latter requirement was withdrawn
however from the two highest Standards in 1879, and
Standard IV in 1880. There was, as has been shown,
a very small improvement in the passes in the
reading examination in the 1860s until in 1868, 90%
of the children were successful. But, the results
were less successful in the 1870s, falling to 86%
in 1877, whilst from that date there was a steady
improvement, until in 1891, 97% of the children who
were examined, passed in reading.(see Appendix II)
The less satisfactory results of the 1870s coincided
with the compulsory attendance at school of large
numbers of children who were not necessarily
interested in school, and who were encouraged in
that attitude by their parents. In Chapter 3 it
was seen that there were too few teachers initially
to meet the demand, and in Chapter 4 the inadequate
supply of efficient facilities was described.

More radical changes were introduced in 1882 when
Standard VII was added, intelligent reading was
demanded of all Standards, and increased fluency in
successive years. The requirements of the Code of
1882 were as follows:

Standard
  I   Read a short paragraph from a book
         not confined to words of one
         syllable.

  II   Read a short paragraph from an
         elementary reading book.

  III   Read a passage from a more advanced

	reading book, or from stories from English history.
IV	Read a few lines from a reading book, or history of England.
V	Read a passage from some standard author, or from a history of England.
VI	Read a passage from one of Shakespeare's historical plays or from some other standard author, or from a history of England.
VII	Read a passage from Shakespeare or Milton, or from some other standard author, or from a history of England.

The introduction of references to English history can be related to the attempts which were made between 1875 and 1880 to encourage the teaching of history in schools; whilst the naming of particular authors instead of the vaguer "few lines of prose or poetry" can be traced to the criticisms made by Inspectoes, notably Matthew Arnold, of the inferior literature so frequently used in schools.(26)

Apart from minor variations in the requirements for Standards I to IV in the Code of 1890, there were no further changes during the Victorian period but in reading, as in other subjects, a new approac to the education of the working people was apparent after 1880. The Cross Commission recognized that "a child who has thoroughly acquired the art of readin, with care has within its reach the key of all knowledge, and it will rest with itself alone to determine the limits of its progress".(27) In 1862 the children were expected to attain a minimum literacy, but the Cross Commissioners, and others after 1860,envisaged the work at school as a basis for further self-education through life, and therefore a continuing growth of literacy. In the 1880s normal children of ten years of age were capable of passing the examination requirements in Standard IV and to do so was vital, for it was widely recognizee that no attainment below this could be of permanent benefit to them. Unfortunately, for many years it was necessary for the Education Department to deplore the fact that too many children passed in lower Standards than what was expected of them, but from 1880 however, this problem decreased, and by

395 it was customary for all children in regular
ttendance to pass the required Standards in advance
f the time when they could commence employment.

The system of payment by results and the establish-
ent of Standards gave rise to a controversy in the
880s that children in schools were overworked, a
laim which was supported by doctors, teachers, and
nspectors. Dr. Crichton-Browne was asked to
nvestigate the matter in fourteen London schools,
ainly in Lambeth, and reported that he had
iscovered evidence of considerable over-pres-
ure.(28)   James Runciman referred to a teacher who
ook dull children to his home and drilled them
ntil 9.0 p.m. in order that they might meet the
equirements;(29) whilst Richard Greenwood,
resident of the National Union of Elementary
eachers, considered that the Code of 1882 had
laced a substantial burden on the curriculum.
arious views in a similar vein were advanced at the
nternational Health Exhibition in 1884.(30) Another
ody of opinion was in contrast completely opposed
o this analysis of the situation, and the views of
unciman and Greenwood were ridiculed by Sydney
uxton, M.P., in his book Over-Pressure and
lementary education; and dismissed by J.G. Fitch,
ho accompanied Crichton-Browne on his visits to
ondon schools. Fitch compared the Codes of 1864,
874, and 1884, and drew the conclusion that the
equirements had not increased greatly in stringency,
roducing the Registrar General's Statistics of
ortality to support his contention.(31)

A scrutiny of the reading requirements of Codes
fter 1860 does not give an impression that
mpossible attainments were expected of children,
nd on no occasion did the examination pass
ercentage in reading fall below 85%. It is
uestionable whether for the majority the accusation
f over-pressure was justified, or whether a scape-
oat was sought for deficiencies of the social and
ducational system. The inefficiency of teachers and
ll-advised educational organization have been
escribed, as have the effects of unsatisfactory
iving conditions, hours of labour, and hereditary
ll-health and illness on the working people. It
annot be claimed that ill-health and illness were
ajor contributors to backwardness, but they were
inor factors in a large proportion of backward
hildren. Disease decreased a child's energy and
ill to master the techniques of reading, and often

necessitated his absence from school, perhaps when some vital stage was being taught. The Code of 1884 stipulated that managers would be held responsible by the Education Department for the care or health of pupils who may have been require to be withdrawn from the annual examination or from some part of school work throughout the year. In many districts managers formed committees of health in which a doctor was usually included, and children were medically inspected, and if necessary withheld from the examination. In 1897 it was recommended that children in ill-health should be educated in special classes with other backward pupils. Suggestions were made that records should be maintained of the physical condition of each child; and systematic medical examination introduce into schools, perhaps as frequently as four times each year. Medical officers were gradually appointed, for example, by the London School Board in 1890, but the medical examination of children in elementary schools throughout the country was not made obligatory until 1907.

Not only could the work of children in poor healt be improved by suitable medical treatment, but also by nourishing food. Dr. Crichton-Browne reported that bread and weak tea formed the only sustenance of many children for long periods, whilst others were entirely neglected by their parents. In a Clerkenwell board school the Inspector discovered that 40% of the children regularly went to school without breakfast, and 28% attended the afternoon session without a mid-day meal.(32) A government return in 1899 revealed that more than one in ten of children in London board schools habitually attended in a condition of hunger owing to such factors as poverty and parental improvidence,(33) and at the end of the century, it was estimated tha 16% of the children in elementary schools in London were under-fed.(34) Endeavours were made by school boards, voluntary organizations, and individuals, to provide meals at a cost of 1d. and sometimes $\frac{1}{2}$d. for which purpose centres were established in a number of towns throughout the country. A noticeabl improvement in schoolwork apparently occurred where meals were provided, but the plan was opposed by those who thought school boards should not be involved, and that it should be the responsibility of volunteers. J.G. Fitch even opposed the latter, for it would, in his view, encourage improvident parents to neglect their children.(35) Frequently

100

e provision of meals did not meet with the
ccess which was anticipated, owing to the distance
centres from schools, the distaste of children
r some foods, the suspicion of parents, and the
thdrawal by other parents of money in the hope
at their children would receive free meals. Local
ucation authorities were not given legislative
wer to provide school children with meals until
06.

REFERENCES

Fitch, J.G., Lectures on teaching, pp.vii, 59,
   60.
Committee of Council on Education, Report, 1844,
   Vol.1, p.141.
Anonymous, Shuttleworth's phonics, Quarterly
   Review, 74(1844), p.28.
Laurie, S.S., Primary instruction, pp.53, 54,
   58, 59.
Ibid. p.59.
Mortimer, F.L., Reading without tears, p.9.
Gill, J., Introductory textbook to school
   education, pp.196, 200
Currie, J., The principles and practice of
   common school education, pp.317-8.
Anonymous, The spell-bound enthusiasts, Punch,
   15(1848), p.250.
Spedding, J., Teaching to read, Nineteenth
   Century, 1(1877), pp.638, 639, 640.
Dale, N., On the teaching of English reading,
   pp.xiii, xiv, 22.
Gill, J., op. cit., pp.204-5.
Bain, A., Education as a science, p.243.
Dale, N., Further notes on the teaching of
   English reading, pp.5, 17-19.
Bain, A., p.312.
Robins, S., Twenty reasons for accepting the
   Revised Educational Code, pp.6-7.
Senior, N.W., Suggestions on popular education,
   p.332.
Robins, S., op. cit., p.5.
Morley, J., The struggle for national education,
   p.22.
Committee of Council on Education, op. cit.,
   1842-1843, p.37;1844, Vol.2, p.503; 1847-1848,
   Vol.2, pp.5, 7; 1858-1859, p.168; 1861-1862,
   p.82.
Select Committee on Education, Minutes of
   evidence(1835), p.20.
Currie, J., op. cit., p.174.

23 Committee of Council on Education, op. cit.,
    1875-1876, p.282.
24 Elementary Education Acts, Final Report (1888),
    p.17.
25 Gill, J., op. cit., p.227.
26 Arnold, M., Reports on elementary schools, p.8
27 Elementary Education Acts, op.cit., pp.135-6.
28 Elementary Schools (Dr. Crichton-Browne's
    Report (1884), pp.3, 4, 5, 11.
29 Runciman, J., Schools and scholars, pp.239-40.
30 International Health Exhibition, Literature,
    Vol, 11, pp.352-90; Vol.13, p.159.
31 Elementary Schools (Dr. Crichton-Browne's
    Report) (1884), pp.58, 62-3, 65.
32 Ibid. pp.8-9.
33 Booth, C. (ed.), Labour and life of the people,
    Vol.2, p.489.
34 Money, L.G.C., Riches and poverty, p.180.
35 Elementary Schools (Dr. Crichton-Browne's
    Report) (1884), p.77.

6 Books in Schools

Naturally the growth of literacy was closely related
to the availability of school books, numerous of
which had been available for hundreds of years. Far
too many of the books were arid tomes, whilst others
had been consciously written to interest potential
readers. Early examples of books which were
availablein the Victorian period, and which were
published in several editions, included Richmal
Mangnall's Historical and miscellaneous questions;
Darton and Harvey's The decoy of English grammar;
Mrs. Ward's Child's guide to knowledge; and Mrs.
Marcet's simply presented books such as Conversations on chemistry, The Seasons, and Willy's grammar.
Interesting as these books may have been, they were
published for use by children of the upper and
middle class, and were hardly relevant to the needs
of working class boys and girls, the average length
of whose school life was only two years in 1851,
and whose knowledge was limited to the rudiments of
reading as well as a restricted, and often deprived,
environment.

Publishers who produced books for use by children
in elementary schools in the 1840s included the
British and Foreign School Society, the Commissioners of National Education in Ireland, the Scottish
School Book Association, the Edinburgh Sessional

School, Messrs. Chambers, and the Society for
Promoting Christian Knowledge. In these years the
latter body issued its first educational series and
selections from Lady Eleanor Fenn's series of
graded primers, Cobwebs to catch flies, which had
been published originally fifty years before. In
1843 James Kay-Shuttleworth compiled The first
phonic reading book, which had the advantage of
having been approved by the Committee of Council on
Education. The Committee was eager for books to be
made available both quantitatively and in suitability for the use of children in elementary schools,
and to this end included in its Minutes for 1847/48
a list of volumes on a variety of subjects: reading,
grammar, etymology, arithmetic, geography, English
history, mensuration, and vocal music. A contributor
to The Quarterly Review in 1844 went so far as to
express concern that too many school books were in
existence,(1) and whilst in general terms this may
have been true, there was in fact a shortage of
suitable works for elementary school children. Very
few, if any, of the books which were available
showed an awareness on the part of authors and
publishers of the reading requirements of working
class children. Neil Leitch's The Juvenile Reader,
listed by the Committee of Council, was typical of
the period, being "religious, moral, and intellectual" in content, and including passages on natural
history, science, and geography, together with items
of a miscellaneous character. The arrangement was by
topics rather than by graduations according to
reading difficulty, and the following extract
illustrates the unsuitable nature of the contents
from the point of view of barely literate children:

> The universe may be considered as the palace
> in which the Deity resides; and the earth as
> one of its apartments. We behold an immense
> and shapeless mass of matter, formed into
> worlds by his power, and placed at distances
> to which even imagination cannot travel. In
> this great theatre of his glory, millions of
> suns like our own bright luminary, fixed in
> the centre of its system, wheeling its
> planets in times proportioned to their
> distances, and at once dispensing light,
> heat, and action...

Even if the pupils were able to pronounce most of
the words, it seems unlikely that they would understand the meaning of this passage On the Creation.(

The five reading books compiled and published by the Commissioners of National Education in Ireland, were written in reasonably simple and graphic language, and were devoted to middle class views of the ideal workman and the benefits he would derive from a life of industry and thrift; retellings of Bible stories and fables; and pieces of geographical and other information. An Inspector in 1853 enthusiastically recommended these books, not only because they were inexpensive, but also on account of their being "best adapted to teaching reading" by means of a graduated arrangement. It is true that the earlier lessons were shorter than the later ones, but attempts at graduation were evident principally in terms of syllables. The Second book of lessons was divided into four sections: words of one syllable, words of two syllables, words of three syllables, and words of four syllables. In view of the irregularities of English spelling, it may be more difficult to read a word of one rather than of three or even four syllables, but this was a point which appears to have been overlooked by those who recommended books of this kind. The readers were unfavourably criticized by an assistant commissioner in his report to the Newcastle Commission, in which he claimed that the style was beyond the comprehension of children at school in the North of England; and he commented that the sentences were too long and complicated for pupils who were unaccustomed to sustained thought.(3)

In the 1850s the numbers of school books increased and were issued by almost every educational society. The standards and speed of printing had improved considerably in the previous decade so that publishers became increasingly involved in the mass production of books. William Collins II issued his first school atlas in 1856, and was appointed as publisher to the Scottish School Book Association and the Irish Commissioners. In a period of ten years Collins supplied the latter body with over 2,000,000 copies of thirty one books. Other publishers who expanded their interests in the educational field in those years were Cassell, Chambers, Constable, Darton, Gleig, and Simpkin Marshall. Unfortunately a recurring shortcoming of school books was their continuing unsuitability for the children on whose behalf they were provided. Some were far too difficult whilst others were boring and failed to arouse interest in their users.

105

Many reading books contained the work of hack
writers and were often "feeble, incorrect, and
colourless". The Gleig School Series does not seem
to have been subjected to the criticism from which
so many other school books suffered, and was
recommended by the Rev. Henry Moseley, a well
respected Inspector of schools.(4) Mrs. Favell Lee
Mortimer's Reading without tears(1857)was also
exceptional in recognizing that "the child will
become wearied by lists of words, and must have
sentences in order to render study delightful". As
soon as possible, letters were combined into words,
and the latter into sentences, which were then
combined into narratives, although "great difficulty
was found in excluding the words that had not been
taught". Unlike the Second Book of Lessons of the
Irish Commissioners, this work included woodcut
illustrations, and as the phonic method was used,
irregular words were omitted. Unfortunately, much
of the text was not very inspiring, for example:

> Tell Nell to get a bell
> Tell Ben to get a pen
> Tell Bet to get a net... (5)

It was deplorable that in spite of the vast
resources of English literature, Victorian children
in elementary schools were provided with inferior
poetical extracts, which were not grammatically
correct and were therefore an obstacle to literacy.
In Chambers' Infant education(1852) the following
verse on intemperance was recommended:

> I saw a little girl
>   With half uncovered form,
> And wondered why she wandered
>   thus,
>   Amid the winter storm;
> They said her mother drank
>   What took her sense away,
> And so she let her children go
>   Hungry and cold all day. (6)

Work by outstanding poets was not necessarily
suitable of course for the teaching of reading. The
S.P.C.K. Reading book for children in Standard III
included poems by Robert Burns, the dialect of which
was explained in footnotes; and by George Crabbe,
the imagery of which was obscure. Various Inspectors
were highly critical of the content of the
traditional reading books, a typical example being
the Rev. F.C. Cook, who complained that whilst

106

reading books for older children were interesting and suited to their ability, those for younger children were "ill adapted to their state of mind".(7) He was generalizing of course, but clearly he had seen books in both categories to provoke his comment, even though other books would have conflicted with his opinion.

Between 1860 and 1870 there was continued development in the production of school books, but writers and publishers appeared to require evidence of increased demand to induce them to devote their attention to the publication of suitable primers. The Newcastle Commissioners predicted an increase in production,(8) and whilst Matthew Arnold was critical of the results of the Revised Code, he claimed that the new system had stimulated the production of an improved and more relevant type of reading book. Arnold considered that the authors of some of the newer books resorted to unnecessary extremes in their endeavour to avoid aridity and pedantry, and introduced "rather too many abbreviations, too many words meant to imitate the noises of animals, and too much of that part of human utterance which may be called the interjectional".(9) Another Inspector agreed with Arnold that many excellent series of books had been made available, but thought some of them unsuitable for the abilities of English children. He complained of several series which were poorly presented and contained large numbers of errors.(10)

The Education Act of 1870 resulted in a vast development in the publication of school books, which was particularly due to the demands of a larger school population and the more liberalized curriculum of the following decade. In 1875 William Collins II purchased the Scottish School Book Association for which he had hitherto acted as agent, because the quantity of business had become unwieldy for a small organization. Almost 1,000 school books were listed in Collins' catalogue for 1875 compared with half as many ten years earlier; and in order to meet the demand additional printing equipment was installed in that year, and again nine years later. Joseph Landon, the educationist, thought that "probably no class of books has developed at so rapid a rate...as that intended for school use".(11)

In 1879 Blackie's Comprehensive readers were the

107

first of what was to become a wide selection of
school books in various subjects, and school
editions of the classics were issued in the same
year. Numerous publishers were engaged in the
publication of school books, and some of them
produced more than one series of readers, including
Blackie, Cassell, and Chambers. Each publisher was
not necessarily issuing new books continually, and
as an illustration of this, no additions were made
to Gleig's School series between 1872 and 1880.
Inspectors expressed particular satisfaction with
Bell's Readers and Nelson's Royal school readers.(12

Although many of the books published after 1870
were well produced, others were still unsatisfactory
containing as few pages and as large a size of type
as possible, and designed to meet only minimum
requirements. The use in books of too many
unfamiliar words was criticized as was the aridity
of content which could not possibly encourage
children to enjoy reading. Harris's First book was
printed, sometimes illegibly, on poor quality paper,
and followed the pattern of the Irish Commissioners'
Lesson books in its divisions by letters and
syllables. In Part 1, the consistent use of words
of one or two letters entailed the inclusion of
almost meaningless sentences:

> I am to go up, if he do it,
> He is to be by, if we do it.
> So do it, if ye go, as we do it.
> He is to go up, as we go on
> So be ye to me, as I am to it...

Part 2 contained words of three letters; Part 3,
four letters; Part 4, words of one and two syllables
and Part 5, words seldom exceeding two syllables.
The latter section consisted of short narratives on
natural history, which were not very interesting to
read. The Primer in John Heywood's series of
Manchester readers resembled Harris's First book in
its use of one or two letter words, and the resulting uninteresting content of the work, the aridity
of which was not counterbalanced by illustrations
of any kind. George Mogridge's The New illustrated
primer, commenced with the alphabet, with each
letter of which a moral verse was associated. Most
of the book was devoted to short verses of a
religious character, but an attempt was made to
cater for the needs of children by the presentation
of the text in large type, the hyphenation of

108

syllables, and the use of reasonably attractive engravings. J.S. Laurie's The third standard reader was far more secular in content, and the inclusion of simple definitions with unfamiliar words enhanced its value, but the use of small type, a dull cover, and only one engraving, rendered it unattractive. In a similar endeavour to appeal to pupils, Laurie's Fourth reader consisted of fables and parables from which the morals had been omitted.

An Inspector in 1879 quoted the following passage from a reading book compiled for children in Standard VI:

> How is one to tell of the rounded bosses of furred and beaming green - the starred divisions of rubied bloom fine-filmed as if the rock sprites could spin porphyry as we do glass - the traceries of intricate silver, and fringes of amber, lustrous, arborescent, burnished through every fibre into fitful brightness and glossy traverses of silken change; yet all subdued and pensive, and framed for simplest sweetest offices of grace.

The Inspector, who was responsible for schools in the Rochdale district of Lancashire, asked: "What Lancashire clogs could guess that in all this cloud of Ruskinesque imagery there is only a description of some mosses on a rock?". He had not seen any series in which the books designed for use in Standards V and VI were suited to the abilities of children.(13) J.S. Laurie considered that "the too technical form in which the written lessons...have generally been cast, has greatly limited their usefulness", and he attempted to satisfy what he regarded as "the first indispensable condition" of arousing interest in his readers.(14) J.G. Fitch wrote that a gulf should not exist between what children learned and what knowledge was likely to be expected of them in life;(15) although another Inspector complained in contrast, that all words and sentences which could possibly present difficulty to children were excluded from school books.(16) When confronted with such a variety of conflicting statements as those which emanated from Inspectors of schools one cannot fail to be bewildered. Nevertheless, whatever criticism may legitimately be made of Victorian school books, the specimens which have been examined by the present

writer were certainly not too easy for the children
concerned.

It was the practice for much of the 19th century
for conversations to be used in books as a means of
arousing interest(see Appendix IV), but the
tendency was for the dialogue to be stilted, and
for the characters to express an unnatural desire
for knowledge. The S.P.C.K. First reading book,
Part 3, consisted of conversations on such topics
as The rat and The yak. Knowledge of the latter,
among other things, was acquired as follows:

> Snow lies on the ground all the year round
> on the tops of high hills.
> Does snow lie on the ground in spots where
> there are no hills?
> Yes. Near the North Pole, which you may see
> in the Map of the World.
> Do men live where there is snow all the year?
> Yes. Men live there, and boys and girls too.
> What do they eat? Can they get bread?
> No. They can not get bread like ours, for
> they have no corn. They eat fish and meat.
> But how can they get meat? Are there beasts
> that live where there can be no grass for
> the snow?
> Yes. There are beasts that live on fish.
> And there is the Rein Deer that lives on
> moss, which grows when the snow is on
> the ground. And there is the Yak, a small
> kind of ox, with short legs, which lives
> on the tops of high hills.
> How does he get his food?
> He digs a trench in the snow with his nose,
> and goes up the hill as he digs. He finds
> some moss on the ground which he eats
> like the reindeer. But by and by he gets
> to a place where the snow is so deep that
> he can not work on.
> And what does he do then?
> He folds up his short legs and rolls down
> the hill till he comes to the edge of
> the snow.
> But what does he do next?
> Then he digs a trench like the first, and
> so keeps on till he has had as much moss
> as he likes.
> I should like to see a yak. What an odd
> beast he must be.

There can be no doubt that well written dialogues

could be of value, especially if they were not obviously intended to inculcate knowledge or draw a moral.

A writer in The Quarterly Review in 1879 echoed the complaint of earlier critics of school books, but with far more justification, that the supply seemed endless on "every conceivable subject", and he queried not only the need for such "excessive multiplicity", but also the principle by which the books were selected. He claimed that by no criterion of selection could one half of the examples he had seen be considered suitable for use in elementary schools.(17) Publishers of series of geographical readers included Black, Blackie, Gill, Longman, Macmillan, and Nelson; and their wares were all too frequently devoid of any interest to children, being crammed with factual detail. A similar criticism could be made of history books which were merely arid epitomes.(18) On the other hand, Jarrold, the publisher, issued a series of Empire readers in the 1880s which was adopted for use in the schools of the London School Board. The series reduced the difficulties of beginners to a minimum by the use of large, clear type, and by confining the attention to words of similar sounds and combinations of letters. A careful graduation of lessons ensured continuous progress, and an intelligent use of conversations helped to produce natural and easy reading in place of the monotonous chanting which was prevalent in oral lessons. Interesting exercises within the range of children's experiences were included.

John Meiklejohn's The Golden primer, which was produced in two parts by Blackwood in 1884, employed the "look and say" method, and assisted the progress of children by a graduated vocabulary, repetition of words and phrases, which were associated with attractive illustrations, and large, well spaced type. In order to increase their interest, some of the lessons were based on nursery rhymes, and the last related to the story of King Alfred and the cakes:

> The King sat by the fire,
>   King Alfred sat by the fire,
> Watch the cakes, King!
>   Turn them or they will burn!
> The farmer's wife comes back.
>   See the cakes! They burn.
> What! the cakes burn! Look!... (19)

Although there is a somewhat liberal use of

111

exclamation marks, the contrast between this and
earlier passages which have been quoted, is evident.
Works with similar characteristics were The Holborn
series of reading books and Cassell's Modern school
series. These and other series in those years
however, contained numerous lessons on animals and
country life, which took "a conspicuous place in
every elementary course of instruction".(20) In the
latter years of the 19th century the experiences of
working class children were decreasingly related to
country life, and were limited to a deprived urban
environment. Their childhood was "one of brick and
stone; its glory consists of shows and shop windows;
and its wisdom is the precocious knowledge of what
can be had for a penny".(21)

    Collins made a major contribution to the Victorian
school book through the innovation of coloured
illustrations which were used to good effect in the
series of Graphic school books and the New graphic
readers. The latter series included illustrations
which were the first of their kind to be illustrated
with pictures in three colours; whilst Blackwood's
The Golden primer and Dent's Walter Crane readers
were unique in that the illustrations were the work
of Walter Crane, the leading illustrator of the
period.

    Having examined the numbers and quality of some
of the books which were available, it is necessary
to enquire into the extent to which they were used
in schools. Where books were provided, it was
normal for the Bible to be used as the text for
instruction in reading prior to 1850. Inspectors of
schools, who in most instances were Anglican clergymen, criticized the use of the Bible as a reading
book, not because it was technically unsuitable,
but because children would possibly read it without
due reverence, and perhaps associate their
difficulties in reading with religion itself.
Managers of schools, frequently admitted the
impropriety of using the Bible in the teaching of
reading, but regretted the inevitability of this,
for Bibles could be obtained more cheaply than other
books. In 1844 a well-bound and printed copy of the
New Testament could be obtained from the S.P.C.K.
for 6d.(2½p), whilst its Fourth reader cost 1/6d.
(7½p). The rules of the Society forbade the
allowance of discounts on secular books, but they

were available for Bibles and other works of a religious character. Whilst this situation persisted it was unlikely that secular books would be introduced into schools in large numbers. It is true that managers of National schools often believed that they were obliged to use books published by the S.P.C.K., but as a consequence of their financial difficulties, advice to the contrary would not result in any significant change of policy. Biblical extracts were still used in some schools as late as 1870 for the teaching of reading.

In the diocese of Winchester, the schools were really extensions of Sunday schools, and an adequate education for working class children in the 1840s was thought to comprise an ability to recite the Church Catechism and to read the Bible. For older children in particular, it was desirable that other books should be provided, and frequently Biblical extracts were used, such as The miracles of Our Blessed Lord and Mrs. Trimmer's Selections from the Old and New Testaments, the latter volume being widely circulated in National schools for almost eighty years. In its survey of Liverpool schools in 1835-6, the Manchester Statistical Society found that the Dame schools were almost entirely without suitable books; and where books were available, they were "of such a mixed character as to defy enumeration", consisting of parts of novels or sermons, and sometimes even political pamphlets.(22)

Only a minority of schools in the 1840s contained books adequate in quantity to their needs. At Cheadle in Cheshire, the school possessed a wide selection of "entertaining and instructive" tracts which had been obtained from the S.P.C.K.; whilst the school at Little Rissington in Gloucestershire was "well supplied with books". A favourable report from the Eastern counties stated that books of an interesting character, containing miscellaneous information, were in use in schools where in previous years only the Bible had been available; and the selections of books in the London area were said to have undergone considerable improvement. Particular series of books were favoured in different areas: it has been seen that those of the S.P.C.K. were chiefly in use in Anglican schools connected with the National Society; and the Moral and Intellectual Series of the British and Foreign

School Society was used in its schools. The reading books of the Irish Commissioners were used extensively in schools in England; whilst a series by the Rev. J.M. McCulloch was popular in the northern counties, and increasingly so in the midlands and south.(23)

In some schools in the 1850s it was claimed that reading lessons were rendered more interesting by the introduction of editions of John Bunyan's The Pilgrim's progress, Daniel Defoe's Robinson Crusoe, and Johann Wyss' The Swiss family Robinson. It was believed that the practice would be more widely emulated if books of this kind were made available at the prices of normal school books; and indeed, the Simpkin Marshall School and home series was designed to satisfy this demand. The Child's story book sold in four parts, each at 2d., and included well-known tales from Aesop, The Arabian Nights, and the fairy stories of Hans Andersen, the Brothers Grimm, and Charles Perrault. In the same series were editions of Robinson Crusoe and Mrs. Trimmer's History of the robins at 8d. It was thought that these books would result in an improvement in the reading of younger children.

During the 1850s insufficient was spent on books, and in one school of two hundred children it was calculated that rather more than £40 should be made available for the purpose. It was not uncommon for two children to learn their reading from one book, and in Herefordshire, a school of seventy six children had access to three torn Bibles. J.D. Morell, an Inspector of British schools however, contrasted the situation at mid-century when in most schools inspected by him the Bible was the only reading book, with 1860, when books written in readable style, upon subjects of contemporary life, were provided. Children were often required to provide their own books, which as a contribution to their education was negligible, for the books frequently bore no relationship whatever to the reading ability, intelligence, or maturity of the pupils. Books provided by parents were often mere fragments, consisting of a few soiled leaves, and in other instances, the cheapest appeared to be regarded as the most suitable. It was ludicrous to expect illiterate parents to provide their children with relevant material without tutorial guidance. Matthew Arnold reported that in many British and Wesleyan schools where books were not provided,

everal children had none. He stated that in his
iew intolerable hardship would result if the
urchase of books by children were made obligatory.
nother Inspector referred to boys at National
chools in East Anglia, who were detained in lower
lasses than was warranted by their intelligence
ecause they were unable to obtain the required
ooks. In contrast he commented upon a boy who was
laced in the top class of his school because his
arents insisted on providing books which were
eyond his ability. Both Inspectors felt that all
chools should possess a stock of books from which
hildren could be supplied in cases where they were
nable to acquire them for themselves.

Unfortunately, the large reductions in expenditure
fter 1862 adversely influenced the supply of books
n schools. The total expenditure on educational
rants in Great Britain from 1839 to 1870 was
12,500,000, of which £52,500 was allocated to
ooks, maps, diagrams, and scientific apparatus.
xpenditure on books alone from the first grants in
848 to their cessation in 1862 was:

	£		£
1848	617	1856	3,957
1849	2,937	1857	7,808
1850	1,878	1858	5,718
1851	1,715	1859	6,145
1852	2,646	1860	4,833
1853	2,895	1861	5,992
1854	1,866	1862	630
1855	2,884		

fter 1870 school boards usually ensured the
rovision of adequate books in their schools; and
n all schools the requirements of the Codes
ecessitated the use of books, initially in the
hree Rs, and from 1871 in an increasing number of
ubjects. Historical readers, for example were
ntroduced into Standards III to VII in order to
atisfy the requirements of the Code of 1882.

The Committee of Council exerted an almost
ontinuous influence on the supply and use of school
ooks. It was evident that managers and teachers
ere generally incapable of making the necessary
rovision and that substantial assistance was
equired. Inspectors appointed by the Committee in
839 were asked to enquire into the funds at the
isposal of schools for books, and to enumerate the
ooks in use under specific headings: reading,

arithmetic, geography, English history, grammar,
etymology, vocal music, linear drawing, and land
surveying. As a result of their findings, the
Inspectors recommended that grants should be made
available for books as a means of ensuring their
liberal distribution in schools. However, in a
letter to Inspectors in 1844 their Lordships did
"not feel themselves at liberty to make any grants
for books". Managers and teachers urgently
required guidance as to the books their pupils
should use, and some recommended the publication
of a list of books in addition to adequate
financial assistance in their purchase. In 1847
the Committee of Council agreed to reverse its
earlier decision, and resolved that it was
expedient to encourage the introduction
into schools of "the most approved lesson books".
It was also decided to prepare schedules of books
from which selections could be made by managers;
and to make available grants to inspected schools
at a rate not exceeding 2/- per child, on condition
that two thirds of the value was subscribed by the
schools. It was intended to amend the schedules
as particular books either ceased to be used or
were introduced into schools. The publishing house
of Longman was appointed as agent of the Committee
for the distribution of books to schools, and it
was agreed that local managers should defray postal
costs. Very few of the recommended books had a
retail price of more than 2/6d. (12½p), and almost
half cost less than 1/- each; and the liberal
discounts which were offered rendered the prices
even more attractive.

   In compiling the list (see Appendix III) the
Committee of Council used as its basis works
submitted by educational publishers and societies;
the prerogative of rejection being exercised on
two grounds:

   1. The unsuitability of a work for
      elementary education.
   2. The book belonging to a category of
      literature too numerous to be con-
      tained in a list.

The Newcastle Commission reported that the
principal classes excluded from the list were
ancient history, ancient and modern languages,
biography, historical and geographical accounts of
individual countries outside the British Isles;

reading lesson books not forming part of a series; and collections of vocal music unaccompanied by instruction. The first group of subjects was probably excluded because they were not taught in elementary schools, and single reading books were excluded because they could not provide the continuity which was possible in a graduated series. The list of books and the capitation grants were found to be of considerable assistance to managers and teachers, but it was regretted that the addition of new books to the former was not undertaken more frequently. It seemed reasonable to many that managers should be allowed to select any books published by educational societies recognized by the Committee of Council, and not solely those works which were listed.

The Code of 1860 continued to permit grants for individual items, although they were greatly reduced. Grants for books, maps, and diagrams were not to exceed 10d. per head of the number of children in average attendance at school, and the total cost of books ordered was not to be less than £3. In order to meet the requirements of the grant, 1/8d. per head was to be voluntarily subscribed by schools, and books must be selected from the Committee's list. Grants could not be raised more frequently than triennially unless the attendance increased by 25%. The reduction in grants for books, to which reference has been made, from £5,992 in 1861 to £630 in 1862 demonstrates the retrogressive character of the Code. The situation deteriorated further when the recommendations of the Newcastle Commission were implemented. A small section of the report was concerned with the book department of the Committee of Council; and it was argued that the Committee could be accused of censorship in excluding titles from the list. Many books were in circulation which contained errors, and were thus unfit for use in schools, but were not condemned by the Committee of Council; whilst others did not appear in the list for the sole reason that its length must be confined within reasonable limits. Criticism was made of the administrative costs of the book department, which had in 1860 been in receipt of £5,683. The administration of this sum required a separate office in Great Smith Street, Westminster, with a clerical staff; and Longman received an annual sum of £1,000 for the collection and

distribution of the books. The Newcastle Commissio
recommended that a general annual grant should
supersede the various special grants, including
that for books, and that the list should be
withdrawn.(24) It seems likely that schools would
be more adequately provided with books when
specific grants were available for their purchase.
In instances where block grants have been
allocated, it has been a frequent tendency for
items which do not seem essential to head teachers
to be neglected, and it has been proved that books
are not always a primary consideration.

In practice the Committee of Council did not
abandon its interest in school books, for in a
circular to Inspectors in 1881, the introduction
was advocated of "a larger and fuller text book,
attractive both in form and matter to young
children". It was recommended that there should b
"a full and well defined amount of content" in
reading books, which would be sufficient for a
year's work; an attractive style which would
encourage children to form the habit of reading;
and a selection of material suitable to children
in each subject of instruction. If six weeks were
deducted from a year for holidays, and a further
six for revision purposes prior to the annual
examination, then forty weeks could be regarded as
available for new work, during which period eighty
lessons, oral or reading, could be given. It was
assumed that reading books for the lower Standards
should contain at least forty sections, and for th
higher Standards, at least sixty, each consisting
of material for reading lessons of "due length".
The apparent vagueness of this term was rectified
in revised instructions to Inspectors which
related to the Code of 1884:

> In determining the length and character
> of the lessons in reading books, it may
> be taken as a general rule that forty
> lessons and not less than eighty pages
> of small octavo text should be required
> in Standards I and II, and not less
> than sixty lessons and one hundred and
> twenty pages in higher Standards.

The purpose of this regulation was to prevent the
use of books in which the contents were so meagre
that they could be learned by heart in the course
of a year, and therefore did not provide an

adequate test of a child's reading ability. An Inspector referred to a book designed for children in Standard II, which he stated was of average size and one of a reputable series. It consisted of 160 pages, but had the index, pictures, and list of spellings been removed, approximately twenty pages of the "yellow novel size" would have remained. This volume would be the reading book of children aged between eight and eleven for the duration of the school year. In terms of the Instructions for 1884, Cassell's New Code reader for Standard I was too short, consisting as it did of sixty four pages, whilst the other volumes which ranged from 112 pages for Standard II to 208 pages for Standard VI, were more than adequate. Jarrold's Empire readers generally conformed in their pagination to the official requirements, as did The Holborn series and Cassell's Modern school series.

In an endeavour to remove abuses the Committee stipulated that two pages were to be regarded as a minimum for an effective reading lesson, and with the exception of Standard I, illustrations, lists of words, and supplementary questions were not to be included when the contents of books were calculated. It was accepted that longer lessons were desirable for older children and it was reasonable for books containing narratives and poetry to be longer than those which consisted of factual information on geography, history, and science. Therefore, all books in schools were not required to conform to a rigid pattern in their length or arrangement, but it was important that subjects should be treated suitably, and the literary unity of each volume be guaranteed.

During the two decades after 1870 an increasing distinction was made between reading books and text books. A writer in 1862 advocated that the variety of subjects which were taught in schools prior to the Revised Code "would be better taught in the course of the reading lesson" from one book.(25) The practice of using multi-subject reading books developed until it could be complained that books seemed "intended to teach physical science, geography, history, English literature, domestic economy, spelling, composition, etymology, arithmetic, anything and everything in fine except reading".(26) The circular to Inspectors of 1881 emphasized that text books should be quite distinct in their use from those employed in the teaching of

reading. The latter were intended to overcome
technical difficulties in the lower Standards and
to present literary variety in the upper school.
In addition to two sets of books required for
teaching reading, another should be adopted for
each separate subject; although in the higher
Standards the subject books would be of sufficient
literary quality to be available for both purposes.
This distinction between reading books and text
books could not be generally drawn immediately, but
the contrast in intention is strikingly illustrated
in the prefaces to reading books at different
periods. In his Third standard reader (c.1871), J.S.
Laurie claimed that "the entire series...addresses
itself to the cultivation of the observative
faculties in particular"; and his Fourth standard
reader was "designed to afford material for the
direct exercise of the moral sentiments and the
reflective faculties".(27) On the other hand, The
Holborn series (c.1884) fulfilled the criteria that
"a school reader should be chiefly regarded as an
instrument for cultivating the power of reading.
At the same time it should exercise the general
intelligence of children, and lead them to take a
pleasure in reading".(28)

The Committee of Council was adamant after 1870
that Inspectors must not recommend the use in
schools of particular books, but it was widely
recognized that managers and teachers still
required guidance in their selection. Inspectors
suggested that publishers should be required to
submit books for the approval of the Education
Department; that the suitability of existing books
should be examined; and that the list of books
authorized for use in schools in receipt of
government grants should be reintroduced. It was
emphasized that the preparation and distribution
of school books were controlled by the publishers
who existed primarily to profit commercially, and
who were not necessarily motivated by feelings of
educational altruism. This opinion was not
unanimous however, as at least one Inspector
considered that publishers could be trusted to
satisfy a demand for improved selections without
the necessity for approval by the Education Department of their publications. In 1884 it was agreed
that Inspectors could "disallow the use of any
books which are plainly unsuitable, or which do not
conform to the requirements of the Code".(29)

That the Committee's policy was successful is proved by a hostile comment from Lord Norton, who detested the complexity of the Code:

The teacher's interest in his work, and command of any special talent he may naturally possess for it, is narrowed within the government groove of minute specification...The very text books in use are advertized as composed "to meet the Code".   (30)

Cassell's for example, claimed that their New Code readers published about 1868 were "adapted to the requirements of the New Code"; and similar recommendations were made for Laurie's Standard readers (c.1871) and the S.P.C.K. Reading book (c.1871). The editions of Cassell's Modern school series and The Holborn series, which were published about 1884, were adapted to the Code of that year.

It is of interest to compare the relatively permissive practice in England and Wales with that in Ireland at that time. All books were provided at wholesale prices from the Irish Commissioners, that is, one set of readers, and books on arithmetic, grammar, geography, and all other subjects which were included in the curriculum. The Commissioners purchased the books in large quantities and sold them to pupils throughout Ireland. The income from the books was approximately £40,000 per year, whilst the administrative costs were less than £5,000. The Commissioners continued to publish their own books as they had done since the 1840s, and maintained a lengthy list from which selections were made by managers. Subject to the approval of the Commissioners, books could be used in schools, which were not included in the list. Inspectors had no power to disallow particular books, but could report deficiencies to the Commissioners. The Irish Commissioners demonstrated that the activity of bookselling by an official body could be organized economically, and it is interesting that the Newcastle Commission, concerned as it was with the need to reduce costs, did not appreciate this.

The report of the Cross Commissioners on the operation of the Elementary Education Acts in 1888 crystallized the attitude of the government to school books, and showed that it had not changed significantly since the report of the Newcastle

Commission in 1861. It was claimed that no case had been established for the prescription and recommendation by Inspectors of specific titles. The Commission stated its opposition to the proposed introduction of a set of officially approved text books. It was suggested that it would be useful for an extended curricular programme to be published so that managers and teachers would be fully aware of the requirements of the syllabus and select their books accordingly. The opinion of the Cross Commission that the number of books to be read in schools should be increased differed from that of the Newcastle Commission. The latter was concerned that the three basic subjects should be taught effectively, and as the content of the curriculum was curtailed, a reduction in the number of books resulted. The Cross Commissioners however, recognized that a taste for reading should be developed, and this could be influenced by the provision of a variety of books. As has been seen, the proportional expenditure allocated to books fluctuated slightly, but never increased significantly, and there is little evidence that after 1890 the recommendation of the Cross Commission was implemented, that a variety of books should be accessible to school children. (31)' Even forty years later, the Hadow Committee on Books in public elementary schools was still able to report that in some schools the tradition of using the three readers survived; and that except in the reading lesson, the book frequently played "an ancillary part". (32)

School boards were often responsible for improvements in the provision of school books after 1870, and many of the members were highly qualified to exercise supervision of their selection. Matthew Arnold considered that school boards were not likely to be condemned for their involvement in this sphere, because unlike the Committee of Council prior to 1862, their activities were confined within particular localities, and only then to schools under their control, and could not therefore represent a national threat of censorship He thought it imperative that there should be close liaison in this respect between the school boards and the Education Department. Arnold was aware of the inconsistencies which would arise if the Education Department continued to allow books to be used in voluntary schools which had been rejected by school boards.(33) As Arnold only made these comments in 1871 it is reasonable to assume that he could not envisage the extent to which board schools would increase, and he was therefore ill-equipped to pontificate on the possible criticisms which could be made of the involvement of school boards with books.

The London School Board found it necessary to withdraw numerous books from schools under its control because their content contravened the rules which related to religious instruction in board schools. A recommendation was rejected that the Board should issue its own text books, but a list of readers was compiled. Managers of schools were not restricted in their selection to the contents of the list, and were permitted to adopt other books subject to the approval of the Board. The selection of text books was however delegated to managers, and for that purpose a list was not compiled. An agent was appointed initially to distribute books requisitioned by schools at a standard rate of discount, but for reasons of economy, a central store was established by the Board in 1874. Publishers submitted their products to the books and apparatus sub-committee, which referred them to members of the Board who were competent to judge their content. Books which passed the scrutiny of the specialists were added to the list. An early decision of the London School Board was to distribute books to children, free of charge; for this was considered to be economically preferable to the organization of a separate accounts department and the appointment of agents to enforce payments from recalcitrant parents. It also represented a conscious endeavour to avoid friction with parents at a time when their support of regular school attendance was being sought, for a confrontation on such a minor issue would not have been justified by any educational gain.(34)

An interest in the guidance of teachers in book selection was manifested in a demand for model collections of school books. Facilities of that kind would enable teachers to compare books of suitable quality instead of being entirely reliant on publishers' representatives, who frequently encouraged them to choose books for the attractiveness of their bindings and illustrations rather than their subject content. The idea was not new, and an early example of a collection for th   i ance of

teachers was located at the British and Foreign
School Society establishment in Harp Alley,
Farringdon Street, London, in the early 1840s.
Collections were established in the 1880s at the
headquarters of the London School Board, at
Dewsbury, and at Beccles. It is not clear however,
what proportion of the collections consisted of
school books, as many volumes were devoted to
teaching methods, whilst others were included for
their cultural value to teachers. Public libraries
were of course able to assist teachers in the
latter respect after 1850, as well as to introduce
them to children's books of merit. Courses in the
use of books and the criteria to be applied in
selection could have been sponsored at training
colleges, but there is no evidence that this
occurred.

It was believed that a scheme of education which
was related to the needs of working people rather
than the teaching of academic disciplines in vacuo,
not only benefited the individual but also helped
to ensure the economic security of the nation.
Increasingly the social responsibility of schools,
the need to co-ordinate academic and extra-mural
activities, and the importance of a practical and
less "bookish" curriculum were emphasized. Books
have numerous advantages for educational purposes,
in that they record material in a concise and
permanent form, and lessons can be revised as often
as necessary until they are understood. Their value
must not however be overemphasized, for nothing can
take the place of actual observation of natural and
man-made objects, and the faculty for this should
be cultivated wherever possible. The Victorians
were well aware of this philosophy of education.

REFERENCES

1 Anonymous, Children's books, Quarterly Review, 74(1844), p.12.
2 Leitch, N., The juvenile reader, p.26.
3 Committee of Council on Education, Report, 1852-1853, Vol.2, p.282.
4 State of Popular Education in England, Report (1861), Vol.2, p.340.
5 Mortimer, F.L., Reading without tears, pp.xii, xiii, 15.
6 Chambers, W. & R.(eds.), Infant education, p.172.
7 Committee of Council on Education, op. cit., 1858-1859, pp.19, 105.
8 State of Popular Education in England, op. cit., Vol.1, p.351.
9 Arnold, M., Reports on elementary schools, pp.104-5.
10 Committee of Council on Education, op. cit., 1868-1869, p.136.
11 Landon, J., School management, p.251.
12 Committee of Council on Education, op. cit., 1880-1881, p.387; 1883-1884, p.253.
13 Ibid. 1878-1879, p.762.
14 Laurie, J.S., Third standard reader, Preface.
15 Fitch, J.G., Lectures on teaching, pp.350-1.
16 Committee of Council on Education, op. cit., 1887-1888, p.352.
17 Anonymous, Our schools and schoolmasters, Quarterly Review, 146(1879), pp.180, 181.
18 Miall, L.C., Thirty years of teaching, pp.11,96.
19 Meiklejohn, J.M.D., The golden primer, Vol.2, p.31.
20 Laurie, J.S., op. cit.
21 Anonymous, The little people of our great towns, Chambers' Edinburgh Journal, 1(1854), pp.55-6.
22 Manchester Statistical Society, Report on the state of education in the borough of Liverpool, 1835-1836, p.18.
23 Committee of Council on Education, op. cit., 1844, Vol.2, pp.223, 520; 1845, Vol.1, p.144; 1847-1848, Vol.1, pp.xx, xxi, 56.
24 State of Popular Education, op. cit., Vol.1, pp.350-1.
25 Robins, S., Twenty reasons for accepting the Revised Educational Code, pp.9-10.
26 Committee of Council on Education, op. cit., 1878-1879, p.598.

27 Laurie, J.S., <u>Third standard reader</u>, Preface;
   <u>Fourth standard reader</u>, Preface.
28 <u>The Holborn series, New reader</u>, Book 1, Preface.
29 Committee of Council on Education, op. cit.,
   1883-1884, p.152.
30 Norton, Lord, "Cramming" in elementary schools,
   <u>Nineteenth Century</u>, 15(1884), p.265.
31 Elementary Education Acts, <u>Minutes of evidence</u>,
   (1886-7), 53,384-53,387; <u>Final report</u>(1888),
   pp.78, 135-6, 138.
32 Board of Education, Consultative Committee on
   Books in Public Elementary Schools, <u>Report</u>
   (1928), p.17.
33 Arnold, M., op. cit., pp.159-60.
34 Spalding, T.A., <u>The work of the London School
   Board</u>, pp.114-6.

7 Recreational Literature

In addition to school books, there was throughout
the period an increasing variety of recreational
literature for children; and an observer in 1842
noted an "abundance of books" for young people in
comparison with the earlier part of the century.(1)
In retrospect however, it is clear that the most
substantial increase in the rate of production of
children's books in this country occurred in the
1880s, and coincided with the growth in literacy
which took place following the Education Acts of
the previous decade:

New Children's Books
(Average per year)

1870 - 1874	319	
1875 - 1879	238	
1880 - 1884	605	
1885 - 1889	455	
1890 - 1892	361	(2)

At the commencement of the Victorian period
children's literature was dominated by moral tales,
frequently religious but always didactic, typical
of which were Thomas Day's Sandford and Merton,
which described the education of two boys under the
tuition of a dull pedant; Mrs. Trimmer's The history
of the robins, which was intended to teach children

the virtue of kindness to birds; and Mrs.Sherwood's
The history of the Fairchild family, each chapter
of which consisted of a story, a prayer, and a
hymn. Less intense works were also available
where an endeavour was made to entertain rather
than to instruct children, such as William Roscoe's
The butterfly's ball, one of the most popular
children's books of its day with no educational
purpose whatever; and Lamb's Tales from Shakespeare. Young people could also read adaptations of
books originally written for adults like The
pilgrim's progress, Robinson Crusoe, Gulliver's
travels, Aesop's Fables, and Tales from the Arabian
nights; but these and similar volumes were probably
given so much attention in the absence of more
congenial children's literature. Gradually, through
the period, an increasing number of books were
written in which the moral was no longer dominant,
a significant herald of this trend being Catherine
Sinclair's Holiday house, published in 1839. This
represented a landmark and recounted the exploits
of two normal children, and although the author
moralized to some extent and even had one of the
characters die young, the entertainment value of
the book could not be gainsaid. Captain Marryat's
Masterman Ready may be criticized for its piety and
eagerness to instruct, and Charles Kingsley's
Westward Ho!for its diet of Anglican propaganda,
but in these and similar books the moral element
was kept in perspective. The period was also notable
for Edward Lear's Book of nonsense, which was
intended to amuse, and although his limericks now
seem rather unsophisticated, there was no doubt
that the author succeeded. Mrs. Gatty, on the other
hand, in Parables from nature, moralized on a
number of subjects, but told her stories in so
entertaining a manner that few could take exception
to her contribution.

By the end of the 1880s there were large numbers
of books available in most categories of fiction.
Boys' adventure stories, which had been pioneered
by Marryat received an increasing number of
devotees; the most outstanding writers in this
category including R.M. Ballantyne, Mayne Reid,
Robert Louis Stevenson, and G.A. Henty. Ballantyne
took great pains with local background in such books
as The coral island, The dog Crusoe, and The lighthouse; whilst Mayne Reid drew on an action packed
career for The white chief, The headless horseman,

and many other tales. Stevenson is remembered for
the exploits of Jim Hawkins and Long John Silver
in Treasure island, and David Balfour and Alan
Breck Stewart in Kidnapped; and Henty reflected
attitudes of the period in over eighty jingoistic
yarns in which he set out to give his readers a
sense of Empire. In the middle decades of the
century the school story achieved prominence in the
moralizing accounts of school life by Thomas Hughes
and Frederick Farrar; the former recollected his
experiences at Rugby in Tom Brown's school days,
and Farrar based Eric; or, little by little on
King William College in the Isle of Man. Thirty
years later Talbot Baines Reed's accounts of school
life were subject to much less moralizing and set a
pattern for later writers. Books for girls were
limited both in numbers and in variety of topics,
for it was far more difficult to interest readers
in domestic affairs than in wars and other forms
of adventure. Leading writers for girls included
Mrs. Ewing, L.T. Meade, and Charlotte M. Yonge, who
described family life and portrayed the social
background of the period.

The decades after 1865 were prolific in books for
younger children, some male writers making a
successful contribution, the most memorable being
Lewis Carroll and George MacDonald. Alice in
Wonderland was completely original and stands out
beside lesser writings of the time, and the
characters in this book often seem more realistic
than many historical personages. George MacDonald's
The princess and the goblin is a delightful fairy
story concerning the adventures of Curdie and the
Princess Irene, and their conflict with goblins.
The majority of writers for younger children were
women who included the highly moral Hesba Stretton
and Mrs. O.F. Walton; and the less didactic Mrs.
Ewing and Mrs. Molesworth, who respectively wrote
The Brownies and The cuckoo clock, which were very
readable narratives. In these years too the picture
books of Walter Crane, Randolph Caldecott, and Kate
Greenaway were a source of enjoyment to younger
children.

Many educationists and members of religious
groups viewed fiction with hostility throughout the
19th century, and it was common for authors to
introduce a factual content into their stories.
Captain Marryat wrote Masterman Ready in order to
correct the nautical and topographical errors in

Wyss' The Swiss family Robinson; whilst Ballantyne described Northern Canada in some of his books; and Mayne Reid portrayed Mexico and South America, submerging as he did so his plots in a welter of geographical and scientific information. Edward Salmon considered Mayne Reid's books were unsuitabl for recreational reading owing to the author's excessive preoccupation with natural history, and he criticized Jules Verne for similar reasons.(3) Non-fiction books for children were available in relatively small quantities; and a selection of volumes in this category which were recommended to boys in 1880 included very few which had been especially written for young people, and most of the books were suitable only for those who were undergoing or had completed a course of secondary education.(4) When the Rev. Edmund McClure became editorial secretary of the S.P.C.K. in 1875, he encouraged his friends who were specialists in archaeology, history, and science, to write books for the Society; and between 1885 and 1905, Swan Sonnenschien published its Young collector series, which consisted of a variety of books on botanical and zoological topics.

It is necessary to discuss the extent to which children's books were accessible to the working class audience; and the fundamental factor is surely the retail price of these books. Between 1835 and 1850, many children's books when first published were both expensive and directed at a middle class readership. Mrs. Sherwood's three volume moral tale, The Fairchild family, was priced at 5/-(25p) per volume; whilst Captain Marryat's two volume tale of the Civil War, The children of the New Forest was 12/-(60p). Less recently published books were cheaper, as were pirated editions from the United States: Tegg's edition of Peter Parley was 3/6d. and Darton's was 2/-; whilst Fenimore Cooper's The last of the Mohicans was available at 2/6d. The prices of these books were too high for working class readers, whose purchasing capacity was in pennies rather than in shillings. It was possible however to obtain slimmer volumes for as little as 1/-, and a relatively inexpensive series was commenced by the Religious Tract Society in 1845, each volume of which cost 6d. or 10d. Books at even this price could not have been easily purchased by the poorer section of the community, particularly during the period of economic difficulty which xtended from the mid-1830s to the early 1840s.

Retail prices rose in the period 1850 to 1875, ut in spite of this new children's books and eprints were less expensive than hitherto. This as a result of new books being published in single olumes; the repeal of the duty on paper in 1861; he replacement of the traditional rag by chemical ood and esparto grass as material for the manufac- ure of paper; the introduction of steam printing etween 1830 and 1860; and the existence of an ncreasingly literate population. Ruskin's The ing of the golden river was 6/- when it was first ublished in 1851, and later reduced to 2/6d.; ingsley's The water babies began at 7/6d. but was educed to 5/- later; and Carroll's Alice in onderland was also 7/6d., later being reduced to /-. Perhaps the outstanding development of the 860s was the production of Walter Crane's toy ooks at 6d. each. During the 1850s, John Chapman ampaigned successfully for free trade in books n spite of opposition from Longman and Murray, as result of which it became customary until the losing years of the century for new books to be btainable at discounts ranging from 10% to 20%. 'his was not of any immediate practical value to he working people, although skilled workers were ore prosperous when in full employment than reviously. Copies of older works became available t prices ranging from 1/- for Mrs. Trimmer's listory of the robins to 2/- for the Bohn edition f Thomas Day's Sandford and Merton. Gordon's chool and home series included The history of the obins at 6d. The tendency to lower prices was vident too in pirated editions from the United tates, and during the 1860s, for example, Routledge produced copies of The last of the Mohicans and Harriet Beecher Stowe's Uncle Tom's abin for 6d.

After 1875, prices of new books remained similar o those which had obtained since mid-century, and ew children's literature, such as Robert Louis tevenson's Treasure island, Rudyard Kipling's The jungle book, and E. Nesbit's The story of the reasure seekers, were published at either 5/- or /-. Numerous cheap series were produced which ncluded Chambers's Sixpenny books for the young nd Routledge's Ruby series. The S.P.C.K. actually ublished a series of penny books which included arious titles by Captain Marryat, but unfortunately the venture proved uneconomic and was discontinued George Newnes' Penny library of famous books appeared in 1896, although in some instances the stories were issued in three volumes. In the years after 1875 working class children were able to buy books therefore, by standard authors, but in general these books were not newly published material.

It was possible to receive prizes in Day and Sunday schools for good conduct, punctuality, regular attendance, and outstanding results in examinations. In 1835 the Select Committee on Education reported that books, both entertaining and instructive, were given as rewards in elementar schools,(5) and an Inspector claimed nine years later that good results were ensured if books of this kind were generously distributed to children. Books were frequently presented to children in the prize schemes which were organized in the Midlands prior to 1870 to encourage children to remain at school. In 1853, for example, of 150 children who competed at Dudley, eleven received £4 each; thirty £3 each; and forty five, books to the value of 10/- each. Many of the children who received money were said to have spent it on books.(6)

In view of the interest in rewards, publishers issued special editions of their works which were intended for distribution at prize giving ceremonies. Reward books were probably sponsored almost as soon as Sunday schools were introduced, and Robert Raikes is known to have distributed books as an inducement to children to attend his school at Bristol. The Religious Tract Society included a list of books which were adapted for reward to Sunday school children in its annual report for 1809; and the series, which was in print for over thirty years, consisted of about six hundred pamphlets. In 1856 the S.P.C.K. published a book entitled The little dog that lost his master, which contained a select list of books "adapted for rewards in Sunday and other schools". Many of the books were extremely pious, and were frequently treatises on religious topics, by such authors as Hannah More and Mrs. Sherwood. After 1870 the R.T.S. recognized the demand for prizes in the board schools, and most of the Society's best selling works were published in the last three decades of the century, including Mrs. Walton's Christie's old organ and A peep behind the scenes.

he books, which were evangelistic in approach,
ere popular as prizes in both Day and Sunday
chools. Reward books with a secular content were
ublished by Blackie, Nelson, and other publishers,
nd among Blackie's successes was G.A. Henty's
Under Drake's flag. As a result of this and other
entures, it became possible for many young people
o possess their own small collections of books.

Children's periodicals of the 19th century may
e grouped into the same religious and secular
ategories as their books. During the 1830s and
840s the periodicals were usually religious in
haracter, and included The children's friend and
he child's companion, the latter being produced by
he Religious Tract Society. After 1850 outstanding
ublications included The monthly packet, which was
edited by Charlotte M. Yonge for almost fifty years
nd was a mouthpiece for her high Anglican views;
hatterbox, which was designed to counteract the
nfluence of some of the secular papers for boys
which were beginning to appear; and Good words for
the young, which for a few years in the 1860s and
870s also maintained a distinctly religious
utlook. In 1879 the R.T.S. issued The boy's own
paper, which upheld a religious tone of less
intensity than The child's companion; and followed
it in the next year with The girl's own paper.
The London press directory for 1877 included the
titles of forty three periodicals for children, the
majority of which were sponsored by religious
organizations.

As adventure stories for boys became popular,
similar periodicals were made available, two
typical examples being The boy's own magazine and
Boys of England. The latter reflected jingoistic
attitudes and set out to interest its readers with
"wild and wonderful but healthy fiction". Aunt
Judy's magazine was intended for girls, and Mrs.
Ewing, the editor, assured parents that they "need
not fear an overflowing of mere amusement". Between
1870 and the turn of the century, a large number of
periodicals for young people was published, the
features of which were "so similar...that to mention
names...would be profitless".(7)

It was customary for stories for children to be
serialized in periodicals prior to their publication
in books. The first stories of Mrs. Ewing were

133

published in The monthly packet, although most of
her work appeared in Aunt Judy's magazine; whilst
many of Charlotte M. Yonge's stories were printed
initially in her own periodical. The school storie
of Talbot Baines Reed first appeared in The boy's
own paper, which was also a focal point for work
by R.M. Ballantyne, W.H.G. Kingston, Jules Verne,
and J.G. Wood. In addition to the work of these
eminent authors however, a great deal of poorly
written material was contributed to periodicals by
literary hacks. Many of the periodicals were
directed at a middle class audience, for at 6d.
Aunt Judy's magazine and Good words for the young
were too expensive for regular subscription by
working class children. The boy's own magazine cos
2d. per week from its inception in 1855 until 1863
when the price was increased to 6d. The publisher
recognized that this periodical could no longer
hope to enjoy a circulation among working class
boys, and in order to satisfy their requirements,
he introduced The boy's penny magazine. Among other
papers which were financially accessible to working
class children were Boys of England and The boy's
own paper, both of which sold at 1d., and Chatter-
box which cost only ½d.

The literature which has been described
contributed in varying degrees to the literacy of
children in Victorian England. For most of the
period there was sufficient material, both in
quantity and variety, to satisfy the needs of all
age groups from childhood to adolescence. Frequentl
books not especially written for children were
found to interest them, and could if necessary be
adapted to the range of their reading ability.
John Bunyan's allegorical The pilgrim's progress,
Daniel Defoe's Robinson Crusoe, and Jonathan Swift'
Gulliver's travels, memorable publications of the
17th and 18th centuries, were available throughout
the Victorian period in editions for young people.
Numerous editions of The pilgrim's progress could
be obtained at 1/-, and in the last twenty years of
the century it was possible to acquire an R.T.S.
edition for 3d. Nineteenth century books for adult,
which were popular with young people included the
work of Captain Marryat, Harrison Ainsworth, and
Arthur Conan Doyle. The requirement in the
Education Department Code of 1882 that children in
and above Standard V should be examined in the work

of "standard authors", also ensured that books by
Charles Dickens and Sir Walter Scott would be read
and perhaps enjoyed as a leisure activity.

There was in addition to the reading material
which has been described, a large class of ephemeral
literature which cost less than the books, and
which compared in price with the inexpensive
children's periodicals. It has been claimed that
the chapbook publications of Catnach, Kendrew, and
others, were in fact the principal reading matter
of working class people, both adults and children,
from the beginning of the 18th century until after
1860. Harvey Darton has suggested that chapbooks
ceased to be read after 1840 as they were superseded
by the work of more competent writers,(8) but in
1849 the Select Committee on Public Libraries
commented on the vast amount of this literature
which was available and read mainly by "younger and
lower class readers".(9) Even in the 1860s the
Seven Dials Press, as it was collectively known,
was still issuing chapbooks at the traditional
prices ranging from $\frac{1}{4}$d. to 1d.(10) The greater
proportion of chapbooks consisted of children's
stories such as <u>Blue Beard</u>, <u>Cinderella</u>, and <u>Jack
the giant killer</u>; but there were also abridgments
of mediaeval romances, a popular example of which
was the story of Argalus and Parthenia, from
Sidney's <u>Arcadia</u>; and other themes of a biograph-
ical, historical, and even religious character.
The Religious Tract Society and the S.P.C.K. were
formed to counteract this degenerate literature,
and numerous commercial publishers produced tracts
on religious subjects in the first half of the 19th
century, including Joseph Masters and Davis of
Paternoster Row. In the provinces the leading
houses were Groom of Birmingham and Wright and
Albright of Bristol. However, despite the activities
of these gentlemen, the working people continued to
prefer the chapbooks, and later the "penny dreadfuls" of Lloyd and Reynolds. Whilst undertaking his
survey of the poor areas of London, Henry Mayhew
examined broadsheet literature which described the
confessions and executions of criminals; and claimed
to have observed instances in Norfolk where two
families would purchase jointly an execution broadsheet for 1d.(11) Edward Salmon, writing in the
1880s, commented that working class boys read penny
dreadfuls, whilst girls of the same class read penny

novelettes;(12) but there was evidence that the
separate stories were being accumulated into 6d.
volumes, which subject to discount, could be
purchased at 4½d. Representative titles included
the spine chilling Maria Marten; or, the murder in
the red barn and Sweeney Todd: the demon barber of
Fleet Street.(13)

In contrast to this type of publication, editions
in serial form were circulated of encyclopaedias,
the Bible, English history, and the classic writing
of Bunyan, Scott, and Shakespeare. Publishers of
this type of literature included Cassell, Chambers,
Charles Knight, Longman, and Murray. Knight founded
the Society for the Diffusion of Useful Knowledge
in 1826, and commenced his activities with a
Library of useful knowledge at a cost to subscriber
of 6d. per fortnight. In 1833 the Society began to
publish The Penny Cyclopaedia in weekly instalments
at 1d. It is significant that when the subscription
was raised to 2d. in the following year, the
circulation decreased from 75,000 to 55,000, and
when in 1843 it was raised to 4d., the circulation
fell to 20,000. Chambers's Journal in contrast,
commenced publication in 1832 at 1½d. per weekly
issue, and maintained both price and circulation
among working people until the 20th century. This
would appear to demonstrate the extent of working
class purchasing power, certainly at mid-century.
At times of economic hardship the situation
deteriorated: Chambers's Miscellany was sold weekly
at ½d. or 1d. from 1845 to 1847, in spite of which
lack of demand among the working people rendered it
necessary for the proprietors to discontinue its
publication. Cassell continued to publish
instructive serials in and after the 1860s at 1d.
or 1½d. per week; and in the latter years of the
century the mass audience was catered for by
Newnes' Tit-Bits, Harmsworth's Answers, the cartoon
strip Comic Cuts, and other popular journals.

During the early decades of the Victorian reign,
daily newspapers were expensive, The Times costing
5d. from 1836 until the stamp duty was repealed in
1853, and the price was not reduced to 3d. until
the duty on paper was repealed in 1861. The day
after publication, it could be obtained at half
price, and was to be hired for hourly periods. The
Daily Telegraph, which from 1855 was the first
national paper to be sold for 1d., was joined three
years later by The Standard. By 1860 there were

approximately fifteen daily papers on sale in London, six of them at 1d.; whilst many more were published weekly at 1d. or 1½d., and it was estimated that almost half of the provincial papers cost 1d. Although prices fell considerably after 1855, newspapers in England continued to be written for and read by the middle classes, and no significant change in presentation occurred until the introduction of the popular press after 1890. Newspapers were, however, reasonably accessible to any working man or boy who was sufficiently interested to read them. As the Education Codes of 1862, 1871, and 1873 required that children in elementary schools should be able to read passages from newspapers, it is reasonable to assume that some would practice reading them out of school.

Traditionally the working people in urban areas obtained their reading material from hawkers or small general shops, and in country districts from chapmen. Seymour Tremenheere, the first Inspector of schools, reported in 1839 that if working class children did not receive their books from "ministers and other zealour individuals" as prizes, they acquired them from itinerant hawkers.(14) Mayhew discovered that in the poorer parts of London there were numerous bookstalls in the 1840s at which books were displayed for sale at as little as 1d.; although many of the books were, of course, quite unsuitable for children.(15) A bookstall proprietor in the 1860s claimed that ragged children waited until his attention was diverted and then stole one or more volumes without reference to their contents.(16) Large quantities of penny publications could readily be found in small stationers and tobacconists in London; and in provincial towns, large and small, they were exhibited "in fruit shops, in oyster shops, and in lollypop shops";(17) and a conteast may be drawn between shops and bookstalls of this kind and the stalls of W.H. Smith & Son, which were established for the concenience of railway passengers in and after the 1850s, and were notable for the good quality of their book stock. Between 1870 and 1900 many young people who would not frequent book shops or libraries, were able to purchase from bookstalls, not only the entertaining or instructive "penny" literature, but also the specially produced periodicals such as The boy's own paper. There can be no doubt that

bookstalls of all kinds exercised a direct
influence on working class literacy during the 19th
century.

Hitherto the reading material has been examined
from the point of view of children who were
literate, but it is also true that its availability
would awaken in children a desire to read. As has
been seen, literature of various kinds was likely
to be accessible to children in towns to a much
greater extent than in rural areas; and in addition
to books and periodicals, children in urban areas
were also accustomed to reading advertisements. At
the beginning of the period, bill posters utilized
any hoardings or fences which they could find, and
sites for advertisements included:

> the boarded fence at the top of the stairs
> leading down to the steam boat station at
> the north end of Waterloo Bridge, the dead
> wall beside the English Opera House in
> North Wellington Street, the houses condem-
> ned to have the "improvements" driven
> through where Newport Street abuts upon St.
> Martin's Lane, the enclosure round the
> Nelson monument in Trafalgar Square, the
> enclosure of the space on the west side of
> St. James's Street, where the Junior United
> Service Club House is about to be erected.   (18

Until the 1860s rival bill posters usually pasted
their broadsides over existing advertisements so
that hoardings "presented the most heterogeneous
possible appearance, and though bills were plentifu
their intelligibility was of a very limited
description".(19) The situation was similar in the
provinces, and under these circumstances advertisements were not necessarily of real value in the
growth of literacy. In and after the 1860s however,
it became the practice increasingly for contractors
such as Partington's and Willing's to hire sites at
railway stations and elsewhere, on which posters
were displayed and could be read without difficulty
Advertising matter was also disseminated in the for
of leaflets, or could be read on placards which wer
worn or carried by agents. In mid-Victorian times
large vans were frequently covered with bills, but
were banned when it was found that their presence
in thoroughfares frightened the horses which were
drawing other vehicles.

It is necessary to our purpose to examine the features in children's literature which made it attractive or otherwise to young people. The fundamental aim of recreational reading is that it should interest the audience at which it is directed. Interest may be aroused through the content of the books, through their physical appearance, and through their illustrations. The popularity of children's books may be estimated to some extent from either an investigation into sales statistics; or the opinions of children as expressed in surveys of reading. Working class children did not normally purchase books for themselves, but acquired them as rewards from schools, or on loan from libraries, and it cannot necessarily be claimed that the books most favoured by middle class adults, were as highly regarded by their eventual recipients. W.K. Lowther Clarke stated of the publishing policy of the S.P.C.K. in the 19th century that:

> Nothing is easier than to deride our fore-
> fathers; but putting ourselves in their
> place we may well doubt whether we could
> have done better. "The Poor" had no
> purchasing power, at least not for books,
> and children's stories were bought by the
> upper and middle class to give away as
> school rewards or otherwise. They had
> therefore to be such as would justify the
> benevolent in doing good...   (20)

A seller of books for children, in contrast, confided to Mayhew that when adults were "really" buying for their children, they selected the traditional fairy tales, or more recent stories in which the morals were not prominent.(21)

In the field of adult publishing in Victorian times, the disposal of 50,000 copies in one year placed a book in the best-selling category, and although this criterion cannot be reasonably applied to the sale of children's books, it is of interest to draw a comparison. The Rev. J.G. Wood's Common objects of the country(1858)was printed in an edition of 100,000 copies, all of which were sold by the end of the first week, and for many years this particular book was in continuous demand. Macmillan was able to resolve his financial problems with the receipts from sales of Thomas

Hughes' Tom Brown's school days and Kingsley's Westward Ho!; and although Lewis Carroll did not elicit any initial enthusiasm for Alice in Wonderland, approximately 180,000 copies were sold in various editions between 1865 and the death of the author in 1898. The picture books of Randolph Caldecott and Kate Greenaway were expensive to produce and were not economically viable unless it was possible to sell at least 50,000 copies of a single work. 100,000 copies of Caldecott's The house that Jack built and John Gilpin were sold in the first seven years after publication; and Kate Greenaway's Under the window was published in an edition of 20,000 copies which was disposed of so rapidly that Edmund Evans, the printer, was unable to meet the demand. In 1878, the year of publication, some 70,000 copies of this book were sold in Britain. The cheap, pirated editions of books by American authors were even more commercially successful: in a period of thirty years more than 7,000,000 copies were sold by Tegg of work by Samuel Goodrich; Harriet Beecher Stowe's Uncle Tom's cabin was published in Britain in 1853 in at least sixteen different editions, and within six months, over 150,000 copies were sold; and Routledge sold about 80,000 copies of Elizabeth Wetherell's The wide, wide world. None of these statistics compares however with those attained by the sales of penny fiction. It was estimated in 1862 that Cassell sold between 25 and 30,000,000 of his publications annually, and in a period of six years, he sold 350,000 copies of his illustrated family Bible. Chambers's Miscellany enjoyed an average weekly circulation of 115,000 copies, although not among the poorer classes. Mayhew was informed that thousands of back numbers of periodicals were sold in the East End of London each Saturday night and Sunday morning, and publishers claimed that 500,000 copies of the most popular specimens of penny fiction were sold each week.(22) Thirty years later it was found that these periodicals were circulated by "tens of thousands week by week amongst lads... at the most impressionable period of their lives".(23) The primary consideration is that the working people purchased these publications and were not presented with them, a fact which is relevant when an analysis is made of the reading preferences of children.

In 1884, Charles Welsh, the bibliographer and

writer, undertook a survey of reading interests among approximately 2,000 young people of both sexes, aged eleven to nineteen, who were in attendance at various schools. The factors which influence the value of reading surveys are many, one of the most important being the nature of material from which a choice can be made, and in the case of the Welsh survey it was restricted to works by standard authors. Another factor is the presence or absence of pressure to which a child may be submitted in order that he will present a given answer, and in this respect, a survey undertaken in a school must always be suspect. The Welsh survey revealed that the most favoured authors among boys were Charles Dickens, W.H.G. Kingston, Captain Marryat, Sir Walter Scott, and Jules Verne; and among girls, Charles Dickens, Charles Kingsley, Sir Walter Scott, and Charlotte M. Yonge. Edward Salmon commented that an option for Dickens and Scott could not derive from a knowledge of their work but of their names, which had probably been noticed in the school library. In this view he was of course incorrect, as the reading of books by writers of that kind had been required in elementary schools since 1882. The opinions of children concerning the work of more recent authors must surely have been uninformed, for it is otherwise difficult to explain their antipathy to books by G.A. Henty and Mark Twain. It would seem that young people knew titles of books more intimately than the names of their authors, for whilst little interest was shown in the work of Daniel Defoe, Robinson Crusoe was claimed by boys to be the book they enjoyed most. Conversely, although Verne was named as a popular writer, Twenty thousand leagues under the sea was among the books least favoured. Some disparity was revealed between the sales of particular books and the stated preferences of children, for although Alice in wonderland and Uncle Tom's cabin were among the most commercially viable books for a long period, they were not favoured in the Welsh survey.(24) It has been assumed by many adult critics that tales in which morals were drawn would not meet with the approval of children, but among girls, The wide, wide world was apparently of greater interest than the less intense family stories of Louisa M. Alcott. On the other hand, a sharp decline took place after 1880 in the sales of R.T.S. publications, whilst those of the more liberal S.P.C.K. increased in conformity with the general trend in publishing.

141

There must presumably have been a point at which
the moral was so dominant that it made a book
unacceptable to children, but it is not possible
to state conclusively when this point was reached.

It would appear that the findings of the Welsh
survey are not sufficiently reliable to facilitate
the formation of any definite conclusion. Perhaps
the most dogmatic comment to be made is that the
young people were aware of work by writers for
adults encountered at school, and the work of
authors of children's books who had attained success
more than twenty years earlier. The most tangible
evidence concerning reading interests of the
majority of working class children is to be
discerned in the phenomenal sales enjoyed by penny
fiction, particularly that of Lloyd and Reynolds.
These children did not only read penny fiction
because it was inexpensive and easily accessible,
but also because the brevity, predictability and
verbal simplicity of its content required a minimum
of mental effort, and provided them with an escape
from the drabness of their environment. The type of
literature thought suitable by middle class adults,
was in comparison of marginal significance. It is
likely that, in view of the unsatisfactory surroun-
dings in which so many of them lived, children
preferred to read short publications rather than
volumes which would have demanded their attention
for longer periods.

It is generally agreed that books which are
physically attractive offer an additional reading
incentive to children. In this respect there was
considerable technical progress in the 19th century
which was closely related to the growing literacy
of the people. Books were first bound in cloth in
the late 1820s, and gold was blocked on it for the
first time in 1832. These features were extended
to children's books, the most popular colours of
which tended to be blue, red, and green, embellished
with designs in gold, and the practice was adhered
to until the 20th century. Reference has been made
to the numerous children's books which were
published in two or three volumes during the 1840s
and 1850s, a format which was hardly suited for use
by children, and was instrumental in financially
limiting the books to a middle class readership.
Whilst an increasing number of books were
attractively bound and were likely to stimulate the
interest of children, the tasteful bindings resulted

in higher prices than would have been the case had paper covers been used. Cloth binding was unchallenged for many years because publishers were antipathetic to the use of less expensive material, and they were hostile to Routledge when he published Walter Crane's picture books in cardboard covers. The innovation was essential if prices were to be kept within economic limits, and the forebodings of publishers that the public would reject cardboard covers proved ill-founded. Although the middle class public was amenable to cardboard covers in the 1870s and 1880s, it would not accept paper covers. Mrs. Ewing's Jackanapes registered disappointing sales in its original paper covers which the S.P.C.K. found necessary to replace with cardboard.

A further feature which could enhance the appearance of a book was the illustrations, and there was a general improvement in techniques of illustration during the century. Initially, the engravings for many books were printed from copper plates and tinted by groups of children; but in other instances, particularly in the case of chapbooks, crude woodcuts were used. George Baxter began to produce coloured prints in the 1830s, and although his process was expensive, publishers such as Darton of Holborn Hill began to adopt it in books for children. The process of photographic engraving was not perfected in England until 1875, and it was used shortly afterwards for the production of picture books by Randolph Caldecott. In addition to technical improvements, more competent illustrators became involved in the production of children's books in the latter decades of the century. The majority of illustrations in children's books published between 1830 and 1860 were aesthetically unsatisfactory, a situation which was accepted by the publishers, who considered that the coarse colours and unattractive designs were popular with the majority of their public. After 1860 however, the superbly coloured picture books of Caldecott, Crane, and Greenaway were introduced by Routledge, who was emulated by other publishers when they observed the commercial viability of his venture. The three illustrators already named also undertook work for children's story books, as did other craftsmen, including Richard Doyle, Arthur Hughes, Sir John Tenniel, Gordon Browne, and Harry Furniss.

In practice, good quality illustrations were

probably no more attractive to children than poor work. Gleeson White wrote in 1897:

> We like to believe that Walter Crane,
> Caldecott, Kate Greenaway and the rest
> receive ample appreciation from the small
> people. That they do in some cases is
> certain; but it is also quite as evident
> that the veriest daub, if its subject is
> attractive, is enjoyed no less thoroughly.(25)

In the 1870s the crude and badly drawn picture books of William Brunton and J.E. Rogers were quite as popular with children as the masterpieces of Crane. The appreciation of art was not relevant to the acquisition of literacy, but the presence of illustrations, regardless of their quality, was likely to arouse interest in children. A scrutiny of children's books and periodicals of the period, reveals innumerable pictures, coloured and plain, which must have surely attracted the attention of young people and led them to read.(26)

The contribution to the growth of literacy of recreational reading was limited, in that its primary function was to interest children, but not necessarily to provide a model of English usage in variety of vocabulary and grammatical accuracy. In all except a small minority of instances the writers were storytellers, subject specialists, or literary hacks, who were not equipped to create impeccable pieces of English prose. Kate Douglas Wiggin complained of authors of children's books who had "neither the intelligence nor the literary skill to write for a more critical audience".(27) It was of vital importance that working class children, who were taught to use standard English at school, but reverted to the vernacular at home, should be exposed to literary influences which would support the work of the educationists.

Although the language of the moral tales, which were published in the latter part of the 18th and early years of the 19th century, was pretentious, it was usually grammatically correct. Mrs. Field, author of a history of children's literature, derided "the elaborate propriety of diction and the marked preference for words of Latin extraction" in which the books were written,(28) but grammatical accuracy and well chosen vocabulary were typical features of books by John Aikin and Thomas Day. It

It is true that Mrs. Trimmer's The history of the
robins exhibited occasional carelessness, but on
the whole, the writers of the moral tales made a
positive contribution to the work of the schools.
Throughout the 19th century, a small number of
authors played a similarly helpful part, and
included Mrs.Sherwood, Captain Marryat, and Mrs.
Ewing. The S.P.C.K. actually published a Ewing
Reader in 1907, which consisted of passages
selected from the writings of Mrs. Ewing for use in
schools. Other writers, such as Ballantyne and
Henty, were so prolific that their use of English
was frequently inaccurate and slovenly. Books from
the United States were often well written, but were
quite unsuitable when they were reprinted from
American editions and the spelling had not been
anglicized.

A feature of Victorian literature which was
detrimental to the growth of literacy was the
attempted use in dialogue of baby talk, working
class accents, and broken English.(see Appendix V)
This tendency became increasingly fashionable in
children's books after 1870, although examples may
be found in earlier periods. The use of baby talk
is exemplified in Mrs. Molesworth's Carrots and in
Lewis Carroll's Sylvie and Bruno: in the latter
work, Bruno's conversation was as follows:

> I went to my toy cupboard...to see if
> there were somefin fit for a present
> for oo! And there isnt nuffin! They's
> all broken everyone...   (29)

Carrots on the other hand, pronounced "nothing" as
"nucken"'. These disparities must surely have confused children with a tenuous grasp of the language,
even if simultaneously they presented their
characters more forcibly to young readers.

Similarly, working class children would find no
consistency in colloquialisms attributed to them by
middle class writers. The literacy of children in
elementary schools could not be fostered by the
pseudo-plebian vocabulary of Mrs. Grimes in Charles
Kingsley's The water babies, the fishermen in R.M.
Ballantyne's The lighthouse, or the London cabmen
in George MacDonald's At the back of the north wind.
It was frequently necessary to modify dialect, for
as Ballantyne remarked in The lighthouse,"strict
fidelity would entail inevitable loss of sense to
many of our readers";(30) and Lewis Carroll thought

that the dialect in MacDonald's Scottish novels was
pleasant, "when one gets a little used to it".(31)
The excessive use of dialect may be compared with
the standard English spoken by the hero in Marryat'
Masterman Ready and by David in Kingston's Peter th
whaler which were published about mid-century.
Ballantyne's The dog Crusoe is an example of the us
of American and broken English accents; and may be
contrasted with earlier books such as Marryat's
Mr. Midshipman Easy, in which Spaniards were
grammatically perfect in their use of English; and
Settlers in Canada, in which Malachi Bone had no
trace of an American accent.

The defects of standard literature for young
people were present and even accentuated in many
periodicals(see Appendix VI). This is clearly
revealed in an examination of The boy's own paper
and Boys of England, which were written either in
sentences which were too short and unrhythmical, or
extended into meandering and inadequately punctuate
descriptions and dialogues. The importance of
grammar and style was ignored in most of the chap-
books(see Appendix VI)and one critic claimed that
the penny fiction publications not only contained
numerous errors but were "rarely legible for three
lines together".(32) Mayhew commented that the
content of these publications was easily comprehen-
sible "in spite of bad grammar",(33) but a
contributor to Blackwood's Magazine in 1898 drew
attention to significant variations in quality
between different publications. He claimed that
some were well produced whilst others were not, and
there were "many degrees of excellence between the
two extremes".(34)

It is perhaps wrong to condemn writers of children's literature for not using correct English in
their work. If the literacy of an individual was
sufficiently established, so that he could discrim-
inate between correct and incorrect spelling and
the use of words, then the better examples of
children's books would present him with a rich
vocabulary and competently written prose. In
practice too, less commendable examples did not
differ significantly from many of the school
reading books which were available in schools
during the Victorian period.

REFERENCES

1 Anonymous, Books for children, _Quarterly Review_, 71(1842), p.54.

2 Ackland, J., Elementary education and the decay of literature, _Nineteenth Century_, 35(1894), pp.416-8.

3 Salmon, E., _Juvenile literature as it is_, pp.35, 41.

4 Anonymous, _Boys and their ways_, pp.204-21, 228-31.

5 Select Committee on Education, _Minutes of evidence_(1835), p.59.

6 Committee of Council on Education, _Reports_, 1839-1840, p.181.

7 Salmon, E., Literature for the little ones, _Nineteenth Century_, 21(1887), p.577.

8 Darton, F.J.H., _Children's books in England_, p.81.

9 Select Committee on Public Libraries, _Report_ (1849), p.83.

10 Anonymous, Chapbooks, _Chambers's Journal_, 17(1862), pp.72-4.

11 Mayhew, H., _London labour and the London poor_, Vol.1, pp.302-8, 315-24.

12 Salmon, E., What girls read, _Nineteenth Century_, 20(1886), p.523.

13 Hitchman, F., Penny fiction, _Quarterly Review_, 171(1890), pp.150-4.

14 Committee of Council on Education, op. cit., 1839-1840, p.181.

15 Mayhew, H., op. cit., Vol.1, p.316.

16 Anonymous, The romance of the bookstall, _Chambers's Journal_, October 1868, p.625.

17 Collins, W., The unknown public, _Household Words_, 18(1858), p.217.

18 Knight, C.(ed.), _London_, Vol.5, pp.33-4, 36-7.

19 Sampson, H., _A history of advertising from the earliest_ times, pp.25-31.

20 Clarke, W.K.L., _History of the S.P.C.K._, p.184.

21 Mayhew, H., op. cit., Vol.1, p.324.

22 Ibid. p.313.

23 Hitchman, F., op. cit., p.154.

24 Salmon, E., _Juvenile literature as it is_, pp.14-15, 121.

25 White, G., Children's books and their illustrators, _Studio_, Special winter number, 1897/98, pp.17-49.

26 Surveys have indicated that children do not

appreciate pictures judged by adults to be
aesthetically pleasing, and are unable to
completely divorce an appreciation of a
picture from that of its subject. They prefer
coloured to black and white illustrations, and
large full-page plates to blocks printed as
part of the text. Relevant surveys have been
published as follows:

Newcombe, E., A study of the appreciation of
  beauty in school children, Forum of
  Education, February 1924, p.1.
Bulley, M.H., An enquiry as to aesthetic
  judgments of children, British Journal of
  Educational Psychology, June 1934, p.162.
Witty, F.R., Children's tastes in book
  illustration, School Librarian, March 1955,
  p.248.
Smerdon, G., Children's preferences in
  illustration, Children's Literature in
  Education, Spring 1976, pp.17-31.

The discovery by Miss Bulley, that children in
rural areas have a greater appreciation of art
than those in urban areas, is particularly
interesting in the context of the present work,
as so large a proportion of the working people
lived in a rural environment in Victorian times

27 Wiggin, K.D., Children's rights, p.86.
28 Field, E.M., The child and his book, p.331.
29 Carroll, L., Sylvie and Bruno, p.39.
30 Ballantyne, R.M., The lighthouse, p.2.
31 Wolff, R.L., The golden key, p.180.
32 Anonymous, The press of the Seven Dials,
      Chambers's Journal, 5(1856), p.404.
33 Mayhew, H., op. cit., Vol.1, p.303.
34 Millar, J.H., Penny fiction, Blackwood's
      Edinburgh Magazine, 164(1898), p.803.

3 Library Provision

There were numerous instances of libraries of varying degrees of usefulness being provided in schools in and after the 1830s, just as there had been for hundreds of years. The S.P.C.K., which introduced lending libraries into National and parochial schools from 1831, levied an annual per capita subscription of 6d., and encouraged the establishment of libraries by grants of as much as £5, on condition that an equal sum was raised by each school. By 1835, the S.P.C.K. had founded almost 2,500 such libraries in England. In 1832 the Religious Tract Society published an address to the public "on the subject of the formation of libraries in schools", and commenced a scheme of library provision to all "well recommended cases", so that by 1849, over 3,000 schools had received assistance in the United Kingdom.(1) When in 1836 the Manchester Statistical Society investigated the educational facilities in Liverpool, it was discovered that small lending libraries were attached to half of the forty six charity schools which were visited; but unfortunately, the source from which the books were obtained is not known.(2) At a local level, libraries were usually controlled by school managers or teachers; and in 1844, for example, the vicar of King's Somborne, a notable

educationist of the period, presented the teacher
at the parish school with a small selection of
books which he requested should be made available
for loan to the pupils, but some time later he
removed them to the vicarage in order to ascertain
for himself their value to the children. In
contrast, the superintendent of a ragged school in
Marylebone reported to the Select Committee on
Public Libraries the establishment of a small
library and reading room which was administered by
the teacher. (3)

Between 1850 and 1870 there is very little
evidence that the development of school libraries
was widespread in this country; and the negative
policies which prevailed in the wider field of
education from 1860, apparently stifled enthusiasm
in every sector of academic activity. In an
isolated instance, a small collection was established by the teacher of St. Martin's School,
Worcester, for which the boys subscribed 32/-(£1.60
the teacher £10, and the S.P.C.K., £5. The reading
facilities in elementary schools were given some
attention in the report of the Newcastle Commission
to the effect that there were apparently few well
equipped school libraries in East Anglia, and in
the south of London they were so rare as almost to
be unknown; but on the other hand, managers of some
schools in Liverpool had formed and maintained
school libraries with the aid of the government
capitation grant. It is surprising that this
practice was not more popular prior to 1862. (4)

The progressive attitude of the London School
Board, which has been described in earlier chapters
was evident in the provision of library facilities.
A scheme was introduced by the Board in 1878, which
necessitated the division of schools into groups
consisting of approximately 10,000 children. At
first, each collection was changed at half yearly
intervals, but four years after the commencement of
the scheme, the groups were abolished and the
period of retention extended to one year. This
reorganization took place when it was discovered
that the potential value of a collection to a
school was not normally exhausted in less than one
year. In 1878 there were 250 libraries in the board
schools of London, but nine years later the number
had increased by one hundred. Inspectors reported
the existence of libraries in board schools in
other parts of the country, for example in various

parts of Cornwall, and at Leeds and Liverpool.(5)
Provision was not of course limited to board
schools, which in terms of educational places only
catered for a minority of the children in attendance at school. It was estimated in 1882 that 16%
of Anglican schools, 10% of British and Board
schools, 9.5% of Roman Catholic schools, and 6% of
Wesleyan schools contained libraries.(6)   A record
of school library statistics was not maintained by
the Committee of Council on Education until 1880,
and the increase in their number was as follows:

	School Libraries in England and Wales	Percentage of Schools with Libraries
1880	2,092	12
1885	3,589	19
1890	4,401	23
1895	6,381	32
1900	8,114	40

These figures reveal a substantial increase in the
provision of school libraries which proportionally
exceeded the increase in the numbers of elementary
schools. The period in which expansion was most
significant was after 1890, an increase which was
probably influenced by the recommendations of the
Cross Commission and a growing interest on the part
of the Committee of Council. However, whilst
progress was made, it was not evenly distributed
throughout the country. In the South West of
England, for example, bookstocks were reported in
1895 as being limited in scope and inadequately
maintained.(7)

The provision of libraries in elementary schools
was sometimes encouraged by Her Majesty's Inspectors.
The Inspector for the Eastern Counties appealed on
more than one occasion for school libraries, which
he thought should benefit from government grants,
quite apart from the normal capitation allowance.
After 1870, the Inspector for Northumberland drew
attention to the cultural deprivation of working
class children, and urged that school libraries
should be established; and similar recommendations
were made between 1875 and 1885 by Inspectors in a
number of parts of the country. In 1894 an
Inspector advocated the emulation of the London
School Board by the organization in other areas of
circulating libraries, and opinion was further
crystallized in the report of the Cross Commission,

when the establishment of school libraries was
strongly recommended.(8)

The Committee of Council does not appear to have
evinced an interest in the concept of school
libraries until after 1880. It was evident that
financial assistance was necessary if effective
collections were to be accumulated, particularly in
rural areas, and the Education Department did in
fact permit the Sheffield School Board to apportion
some of its exchequer grant to school libraries. A
confused situation arose however when the Comptrol-
ler and Auditor General suggested in his report to
Parliament in 1887 that the introduction of school
libraries was not related to the purposes of
elementary schools. This opinion was overruled by
subsequent statements of the Committee of Council,
but its significance was queried by the chairman of
the Liverpool School Managers Committee. Whilst it
was possible for managers to apply for aid from the
Education Department for the formation of libraries
relatively few appear to have taken advantage of
the opportunity.

In 1890 the Revised Instructions to Inspectors
included a request that they should enquire into
the use of libraries in schools, and four years
later the Committee of Council summarized the
situation as being unsatisfactory both as regards
the existence of school libraries and the use which
was made of them. Although the existence of
libraries in 32% of schools in 1895 represented an
improvement on earlier years, much remained to be
done, and this figure took no account of the sizes
of collections or their exploitation. It was stated
in 1896 that "a good school library may be considered as the necessary complement of an efficient
school apparatus, and should be proportioned to the
number in average attendance". The Committee
recommended that teachers should ensure that
children read books suitable to their age and
intelligence; that girls should have similar
library facilities to boys, and have access to
separate collections in large schools with single
sex departments; and that a system of circulating
libraries should be adopted by school boards in
towns, and by a combination of schools in country
districts.(9) When in March 1894, Arthur Acland,
M.P., Vice-President of the Committee of Council,
opened the Hermit Road Board School in London, he
advocated the establishment of a good library in

every elementary school of books adapted to the intellects of children of all ages. He stated his belief that the books which were generally accessible to the middle classes should also be made available to working class children.(10)

As has been seen, school libraries were only available to a minority of children at any time, and before 1870 their influence must have been marginal. Where they existed, much depended on the number of volumes which they contained, and this too was closely related to their availability for use in school or for home reading. Fewer books were required if their use was restricted to school. Unfortunately, statistics are not reliable, as in many instances numbers of volumes are recorded without reference to the numbers of children to whom they were available. Where libraries were provided in Liverpool schools in 1836, they ranged from seventy to 550 volumes, and H.S. Tremenheere referred to a British school in London in the 1840s, the library of which contained seventy volumes for use by almost two hundred pupils.(11) The collections in London board schools ranged from 100 to 150 volumes, but were changed at intervals. In 1900 there was an average of 221 books in each of 8,114 libraries which were investigated, a figure which must have been quite inadequate in many cases. It showed no significant improvement on the facilities of school libraries in the Midlands in 1844, where the collections averaged 214 volumes; or the Religious Tract Society libraries of the same decade which ranged in size from one hundred to two hundred volumes. The assessable value of the libraries varied greatly from one school to another, although intangible influences of particular books on individuals could be as potent in a poorly stocked library as in a well considered, numerically adequate selection.

The function of school libraries was determined by the educational methods which were practised in schools. It has been shown that whilst for much of the period, multi-subject reading books were used in schools, only in the last two decades was an attempt made to provide separate books for each subject; and in neither situation was a well-equipped library required. If project methods had been practised, and the children encouraged to learn by discovery, it would have been essential to provide libraries to support the curriculum, with book stocks equivalent to as many as eight or ten volumes per pupil. In only one instance has the author seen a reference to a school library which was used in curricular activity, and that was at the Abbey Street School in Bethnal Green in the 1840s, where books were "used as works of reference in the general business of the school".(12) Enthusiastic Inspectors, such as the Rev. Henry Moseley and J.G. Fitch, envisaged the integration of libraries into the system of teaching, but in practice school libraries were used for the dissemination of recreational literature to be read at school or at home.(13) In view of contemporary educational practice it is difficult to understand how it could have been otherwise. It can be argued however that school libraries were not directly connected with the work of the schools, and were functioning in a manner which would later be considered within the scope of public libraries. On the other hand, school libraries could be justified if the aim was to develop the reading habit in children which would ensure a continued growth of literacy in adult life. The Cross Commission summarized progressive Victorian opinion in its statement that libraries should be available in schools "as a material encouragement to the habit of reading at home, and as forming important aids to the school course of teaching in securing a taste for reading".(14) At its most active the public library only influenced children who were interested in reading unless they were coerced into using it on supervised visits from school. The school was however concerned with the whole range of intelligences and preferences of children. Informed teachers, and many were not, could help to satisfy the reading requirements of more children each day of the week than would ever of their own volition use a public library. Unfortunately the school library was not accessible during vacations, and if a child was antipathetic to school, this was reasonably reflected in his attitude to its library.

The subject content of the libraries varied considerably. Those supported by the S.P.C.K. after 1831 included works of a useful and interesting content, whilst the R.T.S. restricted its books to those of a religious character, although no objection was apparently made if other material of a moral or scientific nature was introduced. The library at King's Somborne included scripture, history, natural history, voyages and travels, and story books such as Aikin and Barbauld's Evenings at home and John Bunyan's The pilgrim's progress; but in parts of the West Country, the books were said to consist of boring matter far beyond the understanding of children. In the libraries of schools in London, teachers were encouraged to submit lists of books to the Board, and standard literature was included by Dickens, Thackeray, and other writers, together with boys' adventure stories by R.M. Ballantyne and Captain Marryat. Inspectors varied in their attitude to the content of libraries, and whilst some favoured the inclusion of novels, others did not;(15) but it must be admitted that on the whole the opinions of Inspectors were not necessarily authoratitive, for much of the recreational literature which they recommended was not wholly suitable for the growth of literacy though highly satisfactory for other purposes. The attitude that books should interest children revealed some understanding of their needs; but in numerous instances the contents of school libraries at the turn of the century were "as dry as the covers were dusty".(16)

It should not be inferred that where schools had libraries they were available to all or even any of the pupils. The readers who gathered at a ragged school in Marylebone about mid-century ranged in age from sixteen to thirty five, although in the main those who used the library were also pupils at the school. The term "school library" was frequently used in cases where the books were not intended for children, but for the instruction of the teacher; and even where the library was in theory provided for use by children, its availability was often restricted. It was sometimes considered that books should only be loaned to children as a reward for good work, and in the ragged schools of London borrowers consisted of children who were well behaved and had been in regular attendance for at least six weeks. In the board schools of London the use of the library was limited to children in the upper Standards; and the Instruction to Inspectors in 1896 that in larger schools, girls' departments should have similar library facilities to those for boys', suggests that the reading needs of girls were often neglected.

There is very little evidence respecting the

attitude of children to school libraries, and it is
quite possible that many collections were little
used. The same point may be made regarding the
response of children to all aspects of elementary
education. It is possible to cite the views of
individual children recollected in middle age but
these do not really add to our knowledge of the
situation as it existed. The Rev. Henry Moseley
questioned the value of libraries which he visited
in the 1840s, because he was sceptical that children always read the books which they borrowed; but
in contrast, H.S. Tremenheere observed that the
children at the village school in Illogan, Cornwall,
showed a keen interest in their school library;
whilst the vicar of King's Somborne claimed that
spontaneous discussion took place amongst children
concerning the books which they had read.(17) These
are isolated examples of consumer reaction, but
they tell us nothing of the position elsewhere

Many Sunday schools maintained collections of
books throughout the period. The Religious Tract
Society's address to the public on the establishment of libraries in 1832, referred as much to
their formation in Sunday schools as in Day schools,
and it was regarded as quite as important to promote
the cause of education in the former as in the
latter. In 1836 almost half of the Sunday schools
in Liverpool housed libraries; and in the following
decade almost every church and chapel in London was
reputed to have a collection.(18) Whilst there is
not a great deal of information available, it seems
evident that about 1860 Sunday schools often
possessed superior libraries to Day schools; and in
East Anglia, for example, where Day school libraries
were rare, almost every Sunday school contained a
library, which was usually well used.(19) Where
Sunday school libraries existed, their influence
was potentially great, for it was customary for
young people to remain associated with their local
Sunday schools until they reached the age of
eighteen or twenty. As a considerable proportion of
children prior to 1870 never attended Day schools,
it follows that Sunday schools with libraries had
a positive role to fulfil in their education.

As with Day school libraries, those in Sunday
schools varied in size and content. After 1850
their importance slowly declined as public libraries

developed, although they remained influential in rural areas. It is perhaps reasonable that most of the libraries contained material of a religious character, but in fact some included secular books of voyages and travels. A book devoted to advice on the organization of Sunday schools in 1835, recommended that books should "invariably be upon religious subjects",(20), and indeed there was good reason for the availability of so much pious literature, quite apart from the religious function of the schools. The principal sources from which books were obtained were the R.T.S., the Sunday School Union, and the S.P.C.K. During the latter years of the century the moral intensity of the publications of the two former organizations was seen to relax, and the S.P.C.K. had been responsible for books on a wide range of topics for many years. These bodies did however produce inexpensive, pious tracts, and owing to the availability of insufficient funds, it was this material which tended to be favoured by Sunday school teachers for inclusion in their libraries.

Thomas Greenwood, a leading librarian of the period, suggested that Sunday school libraries should include books on history, natural history, science, and travel, and works of good quality fiction. He appreciated that the aim of Sunday school collections must be to foster the moral and intellectual nature of readers, but did not consider that this was often affected by books "in which the name of the Almighty appeared profusely on every page". Although Greenwood did not refer specifically to writers of children's books, many of them were represented in the list of over four hundred works which formed an appendix to his book on Sunday school libraries.(21) In instances where Sunday school teachers modelled their libraries on his ideas, there can be no doubt that the collections would be well patronized, and be one of the few sources from which working class children could acquire good quality reading material.

It would be impossible to determine the extent to which Sunday school libraries were provided for the use of children, and the growth of literacy in young people was not necessarily assisted by their existence. In some instances contemporary records show that libraries were in fact used by children. A reading room, for example, was attached to the Liverpool Domestic Mission's Tuckerman Institute in

1850, which was open each evening and was visited by approximately one hundred young people, who borrowed material for home reading. The libraries which were located in Sunday schools in Cheshire and Lancashire in the 1870s however, were stocked with books, the majority of which were intended for adults, and only incidentally of interest to children. Collections were frequently restricted to use by teachers, many of whom were enthusiastic in their religious beliefs, but possessed insufficient Biblical knowledge or reading ability. A balanced teachers' collection would include books on educational aims and methods, elementary works on specific subjects taught at the school, and a selection of reference books.

Sunday schools frequently organized reading circles in the latter decades of the century, with the assistance of the Victoria Reading Circle of the Sunday School Union, the value of which was endorsed by the Committee of Council, and which included a section for young people, and co-operated with Sunday schools in their reading programmes. The programme of the section in 1891/92 included the reading of secular literature, either individually or in groups; and amongst the recommended books were Dickens' A Christmas carol; Hawthorne's Tanglewood tales; Longfellow's narrative poems; histories by Mandell Creighton and S.R. Gardiner; and some biography and miscellaneous literature. The books in the selection were generally well written, and whilst most were not produced specifically for young people, they were likely to interest them.

School libraries of all kinds were basically unstable in that they usually owed their existence to the initiative of individuals, which was insufficient to ensure their continuance. Although the vicar of King's Somborne was responsible for the formation of a highly successful library, there is no evidence to suggest that his successor manifested any interest in the work. The only satisfactory opportunity for continuity was in instances where the libraries were maintained or supported by corporate bodies such as the R.T.S. or the S.P.C.K. from 1831; public libraries after 1850; or school boards from 1870. The managers of many, perhaps most voluntary schools, could not compete with the more progressive school boards as regards the provision of libraries, and consequently

the majority of children were deprived of adequate
reading facilities in their schools. Where adequate
financial support was available however, the
teacher exercised the principal influence on the
use by children of the school library. A teacher's
commitment to the cause of school libraries was
dependent on his previous experience of books at
home and at school, or during his period of training. There is little evidence that books were
likely to play an important part in any of these
situations during the Victorian period.

Very few library facilities were available to
working class children prior to 1850, apart from
those which were provided by Day and Sunday schools.
It is true that some provision was made in the
libraries of mechanics' institutes, but Samuel
Smiles, the promoter of self-help, informed the
Select Committee on Public Libraries in 1849 that
the mechanics' institutes in the large towns were
usually frequented by "the middle and respectable
classes", whilst only "a small proportion of working men receiving comparatively high wages"
supported the institutions.(22) During the 1840s
mutual improvement societies were formed by groups
of young men in various parts of the country,
because they could not afford the weekly fee of 3d.
or 4d. which was required by mechanics' institutes.
At Uxbridge, three evenings were devoted each week
to reading from 6.30 p.m. to 10.0 p.m., and on
other evenings, part of the time was devoted to
this activity. The members paid 2d. per week and
subscribed to such periodicals as The Illustrated
London News, The News of the World, Chambers's
Journal, and about thirty other journals. A
similar society at Hampstead enjoyed much the same
kind of facilities and was supported by gardeners,
young journeymen, and the sons of village tradesmen, but it was regretted that there were in the
neighbourhood "hundreds of sandboys, donkey boys,
and other youths" who could not become members.(23)
In addition to groups of this kind, there were also
instances of libraries or facilities for reading
being provided by local clergy, but which seldom
survived for long periods.

In 1850, the Public Libraries Act made it possible
for local government areas with populations exceeding 10,000 to become library authorities if they so
wished. The rate which could be levied for the

provision and maintenance of the libraries was
limited to $\frac{1}{2}$d. in the £, and admission was to be
free. No provision was made for the purchase of
books, as it was considered that adequate donations
of material would be made. This Act was superseded
five years later, and the new legislation stipulated that the population limit should be reduced to
5,000, and the rate increased to 1d., and authorized the purchase, provision, and repair of books.
In view of the financial limitations, and the small
populations on whose behalf the Act could be
adopted, it is not surprising that by 1859 only
twenty one local authorities had availed themselves
of their powers. The Public Libraries Acts were
amended on numerous occasions between 1866, when
the population limit was removed, and 1890, and
were consolidated in 1892.

The growth of public libraries was accelerated
after the passing of the Elementary Education Acts
of the 1870s. At the opening ceremony of the library
which was to serve the Nottinghamshire villages of
Carlton and Hucknall Torkard, a local worthy
expressed the view that the new service was a
necessary consequence of the growth of literacy,
and was the only means of ensuring that the young
people of the district had an opportunity to
·increase their knowledge after they had lest
school.(24) This opinion was not apparently
reflected in all parts of Britain, for as late as
1896, forty six districts with populations of more
than 20,000 had refused to adopt the Public
Libraries Act. Opposition was particularly evident
in London, where with the exception of eleven
districts which adopted the Act in commemoration of
the Jubilee of Queen Victoria in 1887, activity in
this respect was not widespread until the closing
years of the century.

The earliest known example of a service being
provided for young people in a rate supported
library was at Manchester in 1862, when a separate
reading department for boys with its own stock of
suitably selected literature was established. The
facilities were made available owing to the heavy
use of the library by unemployed workers during the
economic depression which was eventually aggravated
by the cotton famine resulting from the Civil War
in the United States. Special collections of
children's books were set up at Birkenhead in 1865
and at Birmingham in 1869, but whilst the idea was

praiseworthy, the numbers of books were quite inadequate to satisfy any appreciable demand. There were about 69,000 children in Birmingham at that time, a community which could not possibly take advantage of the four hundred or so books allocated for their use in the library. Notable examples of library work with young people after 1870 were at Cambridge from 1872, Plymouth from 1879, Nottingham from 1882, and Bootle from 1891. By 1898 however, only 108 out of more than 300 libraries in England and Wales had made provision for young people; and fewer than forty had separate rooms for children.(25) Various librarians were genuinely concerned with the need to make available books for children, and to this end established sections for their use. The librarian of Plymouth for example, discovered that it was not sufficient to provide a collection of books, no matter how well selected, if the children did not receive some guidance. He believed it to be important to foster a love of reading for both information and recreation in children, who, owing to the poverty of their home environment had very little acquaintance with books. If the library was also as attractive as possible in its decoration and atmosphere, the children would be further encouraged to use its facilities.(26) Other librarians considered that books for children should be located, not in the public library, but in the elementary school.

There was no uniformity in the conditions by which children could become members of public libraries. In most cases both boys and girls were allowed access to the facilities, but in some instances, as at Manchester and Chelsea, the service was restricted to boys. Many libraries had a minimum age requirement ranging from twelve to sixteen years, and the following table shows variations in practice which existed in this respect:

Bootle	8 - 15	
Cambridge	8 - 14	
Nottingham	7 - 14	

Rules were framed to ensure the good behaviour of children and the responsible treatment by them of public property. Parents or guardians were expected to act as guarantors before the children could be admitted to the library, a rule which served to exclude many potential readers because the parents of poorer children were often unwilling to satisfy

this condition. Rules regarding the physical
cleanliness of children were necessary, but in the
absence of washing amenities in the library, many
young people from slum areas were refused membership. It follows that the organization of libraries for children was favourable to the middle and
respectable working classes. Those who could
benefit most in relation to the extent of their
social disabilities were rejected by public
libraries as they had been by most other sectors
of society.

In some libraries it was possible for young
people to use the adult lending department when
they had attained a stipulated age, and in the
absence of special facilities. At the end of the
century, the minimum age for membership at Penge
was fourteen; at Stoke Newington, ten; and at
Willesden Green, eight or nine. The librarian of
Willesden Green commented that "so much good might
be accomplished by making the rule respecting the
age for admission more elastic".(27) On the other
hand, in view of the slow growth in literacy, it is
not surprising that many librarians did not
consider it important to extend adult facilities
to young people. However, the movement grew in
public libraries to lower the age limit for use of
adult departments and so give access to those who
could profit thereby. At Nottingham the minimum age
limit had remained static at fourteen years since
1867, but in 1900 it was reduced to thirteen. Thus
young people could graduate from the children's
library when they had exhausted its contents.
Similar relaxations were made at Chester from
twelve to ten; Hammersmith, thirteen to eleven; and
Kilburn, fourteen to twelve. This did not of course
recognize that some children mature more quickly
than others of the same age, but nevertheless
represented a desire on the part of librarians to
come to terms with the reading requirements of
young people.

Few records exist of the actual contents of
children's libraries in Victorian times. At Manchester in the 1860s the books included The Arabian
nights, Aesop's Fables, Robinson Crusoe, and
Charles Dickens' A child's history of England. A
detailed account was given by the librarian of
Nottingham of the contents of his children's
library, approximately half of his stock consisting
of fiction; and the names of most of the well known

uthors were included, many of their works being
uplicated. He excluded books on philosophy and
hilology, and only provided theological works
very sparingly and selected with great care".
ooks on chemistry and natural history were well
epresented.(28) <u>The catalogue of books for the
oung</u>,first published by the Bootle public library
n 1891, is an impressive commentary on the
esources of a well stocked library. In the first
dition of over 1,000 volumes were listed, many of
hich were not written specifically for children,
uch as works by H. Rider Haggard, Jerome K. Jerome,
nd Annie S. Swan. In view of the limited financial
esources which were available to public libraries,
t is of interest that the catalogue contained such
ecent publications as Robert Louis Stevenson's
<u>he master of Ballantrae</u>(1889) and Andrew Lang's
<u>ed fairy book</u>(1890).

During the Victorian period few children were
llowed direct access to books in public libraries,
nd in this respect, school libraries had obvious
dvantages. Children were expected to rely on
atalogues which ranged from simple lists to well
roduced printed publications, and it was not
ncommon for them to choose books by their titles,
nd after a brief scrutiny to return them
nread.(29) The advantage of a competent staff to
ssist users could not under these circumstances be
inimized, for the small amount of information
hich it is possible to include in a catalogue
ntry is usually insufficient for the satisfactory
election of books. Specialist staff were rare, and
nsuitable requests both in content and relevance
ere made simply because of this inherent limitat-
on. The earliest instance in which borrowers, not
ecessarily children, were allowed to consult books
t the shelves of a library was not until 1894 at
lerkenwell. Emulation of this innovation of "open
ccess" was slow, owing to the expense involved in
he removal of elaborate fittings and the subsequent
nstallation of new equipment. Although young
eople required guidance in the consultation of
atalogues, it was imperative if they obtained
ccess to the bookshelves. There was not however
staff of librarians which was competent to assist
hem in the location of books which would be of
nterest to them, suitable to their reading
bility, and written in a manner which would
ontribute to their literacy.

Public libraries sometimes established collectio:
of books in schools, the first known instances of
such co-operation being at Leeds in 1884 and
Plymouth in 1888. Whilst the rooms were regarded a,
public library branches, they were in fact intende
for use by the children in attendance at the board
schools. Between 1885 and the end of the century
schemes of public library/school co-operation were
initiated in various parts of the country, but the
concept had its opponents. Some teachers were not
enthusiastic to have collections of books in their
schools which they were expected to administer,
although they were often prepared to encourage
children in the use of the public library. Opinion
among librarians was divided, and some thought tha
neither board schools should be used for library
purposes, nor teachers invited to supervise the
reading of their pupils.(30) A potentially explosi
situation arose when the town clerk of Folkestone
decided that it was illegal for a library authority
to provide books from the public library for the
exclusive use of a particular group. The practice
was never challenged in a court of law, but the
point of interest lies in the eagerness of the
opponents of school libraries to invoke the law in
an attempt to avoid possible expenditure. The most
vital factor was probably that of finance, and
whilst this could be regarded as an excuse for
failure to provide a library service to schools, i
certainly had validity. At Leeds the collections
were well used, and it was found impossible to
maintain them; and after complaints of damage to
the books at Norwich the scheme there was discontinued. School boards, allowed as they were to
provide grants for libraries in schools, were in a
more advantageous position in this respect than wer
public libraries. The principal disadvantage of
complete school board control was the removal of
opportunity for co-operation, and a consequent
failure to provide the bridge which was necessary
if young people were to continue the habit of
reading at the conclusion of their formal education
Various agreements were reached as to the administration of the libraries: at Leeds and Plymouth the
books were purchased from the income of the public
library, whilst the school board assumed responsibility for the fittings. With very few exceptions
all costs were met by the public library committees
at first, and it became clear that joint schemes
could only be successful if the school board was

repared to allocate grants.

The closest co-operation was desirable between ibrarians and teachers in the guidance of children s to their choice of reading. Although a teacher new and could influence children to a greater xtent than a librarian, by virtue of his more requent and personal contact with them, it fell o the librarian to select suitable books and to rganize them into a helpful arrangement. It was onsidered by some to be the responsibility of a hild's parents to direct the course of his eading, but as has been seen, so many parents were nable to carry out this duty owing to their own ack of education and literary experience. In these ircumstances the librarian and the teacher were xpected to undertake the task, and their competence or this must be queried. In many instances children orrowed books from public libraries for no other eason than that their physical appearance was nviting. Where libraries were large and busy it was xtremely difficult to supervise children adequat- ly, and the solution of the problem seemed to have een found if small collections of books, approved y librarians and teachers, were placed in schools.

In 1896 the Committee of Council on Education ecommended that children should be made aware of he facilities offered by the public library, and uggested that this could be accomplished by means f visits and talks.(31) The unfortunate situation hich existed as a result of the inadequate finances vailable to public libraries was not aggravated by ibrarians giving talks to school children on ibrary premises. An agreement was reached, for xample, between the librarian of Cardiff and head eachers of board and voluntary schools, that pupils n Standards IV to VII should visit the public ibrary once in each year for a talk by the ibrarian. The Committee of Council commented avourably on the many instances in which closer ontact was developed between public libraries and lementary schools.(32)

If elementary schools and public libraries were o be regarded as complementary contributors to the ational level of literacy, it would seem reasonable o suggest that both organizations should have been esponsible to the same department, both locally nd nationally, and that each should have maintained standards which recognized the functions of the ther. It is true that the efficacy of this develop-

165

ment must have been influenced by the range of
books which was available to children, but after
1860 the numbers of both school books and recreational reading increased considerably. As has been
seen, the principal deficiency in the range of
available material was in the category of general
non-fiction, and for this reason, public library
collections were drawn from works written for
adults by standard writers of biography, history,
science, and travel. This situation resulted from
the concentration on text book methods in schools,
and it would be reasonable to suppose that a movement to active learning and the consequent need for
a wide range of non-fiction, would have made it
economically feasible for publishers to produce
specially written factual literature for children.
A trend of this kind would have been reflected on
the shelves of public libraries and would have
served to demonstrate the essential relationship
between their functions with that of formal
education. Without the imposition of standards on
publishers however, the deficiencies in books which
have been discussed would almost certainly have
remained as an obstacle to the growth of literacy,
and both teachers and librarians would have found
it necessary to exercise a policy of selection
which many of them were not qualified to undertake

REFERENCES

1   Select Committee on Public Libraries,
    Report(1849), pp.168-9.
2   Manchester Statistical Society, Report on the
    state of education in the borough of Liver-
    pool in 1835-1836, p.vi.
3   Select Committee on Public Libraries, op. cit.,
    p.207.
4   State of Popular Education in England,
    Report(1861), Vol.3, pp.315, 539; Vol.4,p.376.
5   Committee of Council on Education, Reports,
    1879-1880, p.248; 1881-1882, p.318; 1883-1884,
    p.328.
6   Library Association Monthly Notes, 4, 15th
    September 1883, p.116.
7   Committee of Council on Education, op. cit.,
    1894-1895, p.17.
8   Ibid. 1853-1854, Vol.2, p.313; 1854-1855,
    p.476; 1875-1876, p.379; 1879-1880, pp.224,
    248, 385; 1881-1882, pp.305, 318; 1883-1884,
    p.328.
9   Ibid. 1895-1896, p.443.
10 Anonymous, Library notes and news, Library,
    6(1894), p.124.
11 Committee of Council on Education, op. cit.,
    1842-1843, p.477.
12 Ibid. p.449.
13 Ibid. 1844, Vol.2, p.522; 1846, p.110.
14 Elementary Education Acts, Final Report(1888)
    p.136.
15 Committee of Council on Education, op. cit.,
    1875-1876, p.379.
16 Ibid. 1897-1898, p.217.
17 Ibid. 1840-1841, p.193; 1842-1843, p.457;
    1844, Vol.2, pp.103, 521.
18 Select Committee on Public Libraries, op. cit.,
    pp.168, 169, 172.
19 State of Popular Education in England, op. cit.,
    Vol.3, pp.225, 315.
20 Sunday School Society of Ireland, Hints for
    conducting Sunday schools, pp.128-9.
21 Greenwood, T., Sunday school and village
    libraries, pp.8, 10, 59.
22 Select Committee on Public Libraries, Minutes
    of Evidence(1849), p.124.
23 Anonymous, Working men's evenings: the Hampstead
    reading rooms, Chambers's Edinburgh Journal
    March 1846, p.175.

24 Greenwood, T., Public libraries, 1890 ed.,p.157

25 Greenwood, T.,(ed.), Library year book, 1900-
1901, p.269.

26 Wright, W.H.K., The public free library and the
board school, Library Association, Transactions and proceedings of the annual meeting,
1879, p.40

27 Chennell, F.C., The public library age limit,
Library World, 2(1900), pp.175-6.

28 Briscoe, J.P., Libraries for the young,
Library Chronicle, 3(1886), pp.46-7.

29 Edwards, E., Free town libraries, p.80.

30 Wright, W.H.K., op. cit., p.96(Discussion).

31 Committee of Council on Education, op. cit.,
1895-1896, p.443.

32 Ibid. 1897-1898, p.20.

9 Conclusion

Before 1870, parents were probably the strongest
influence on whether or not working class children
attended school, although where the attitude of
parents was negative this may have been the result
of pressures on them by insensitive employers or
the need for some additional income to avoid the
misery of poverty and all that this implied.
Parents who sacrificed the potential income of
their children in order that they might be educated
were then faced with the problem of providing them
with the fees, and even text books, which were
required by schools, and clothing them to a
minimum level of decency.

It was possible for newly married couples to
maintain a reasonable standard of living during
periods of high employment, but the relative
prosperity was increasingly eroded as the size of
the family increased. Inevitably the situation was
reached that if for one reason or another it was
decided to send children to school, then it would
not be possible to give such essentials as food,
clothing, and warmth, the priority of the family
budget which they must have if malnutrition and
general ill-health were to be kept at a distance.
Conditions at home were in any case likely to be
detrimental to health, and all who were exposed to

such a situation were prey to every passing
epidemic; whilst at work an insanitary environment
was often combined with the specific hazards of
factory labour, which were debilitating and a
threat to life and limb. In country districts,
cottages tended to be damp, the walk to and from
work in all weathers could be long, and the day's
work exhausting. Children were sent to school
physically incapable of coping with the rigours of
the curriculum; and if they were engaged for part
of the day in manual employment, their personal
ability to benefit from education was considerably
reduced.

Parents with very little or no educational
background were not well placed to give children
the mental stimulus which would support their
progress in school. Whilst it would be naive to
assume that illiterate parents could not communicate
with their children at all, it is reasonable to
suggest that with poor vocabularies they would be
unable to use the spoken word as a means of precise
communication, or as a vehicle for interesting
conversation. It is unlikely that, in the towns at
least, there would be many books in the home, apart
perhaps from the Bible, and small quantities of
chapbook and other ephemeral literature. There was,
during the period, a gradual improvement in the
living standards, certainly of skilled workers,
and to a lesser extent unskilled workers, and real
wages were substantially higher in 1901 than they
had been at mid-century. The pressures on parents
which had for so long militated against children
being sent to school gradually decreased; whilst at
the same time coercive measures were taken, albeit
inadequately, to ensure that the employment of
young people should be restricted, and that they
should attend school, not erratically, but for a
length of time which would result in the attainment
of literacy.

The Victorian period is conveniently bounded by
two notable educational developments: in 1833 the
first Parliamentary grant was made to the voluntary
National and British and Foreign School Societies;
and in 1902 the Education Act effected the transfer
of educational powers to local authorities, and the
closer co-ordination of elementary and secondary
education. Approximately mid-way through the period,
in 1870, progress was marked by the establishment of
the system of dual control; and school boards were

set up to make provision for elementary instruction in numerous parts of the country not already served in this respect by voluntary bodies. The rise in the school population during the sixty or more years of Victoria's reign, and the major legislative landmarks of the era, give a superficial impression of continuous progress, which is of course misleading. The Revised Code of 1862, the outcome of the deliberations of the economy orientated Newcastle Commission, constituted a serious setback to the evolutionary process, for the variable character of the new grant undermined the stability of schools, and its pernicious effects were to be felt until the 1890s. There can be no doubt that the Newcastle Commissioners in their investigations found few schools to be adequate, owing on the one hand to the irregular attendance of children at school, and on the other, to the incompetence of teachers who were all too frequently lacking in technical expertise, cultural attainments, and even literacy itself.

However, confronted with the system of payment on the basis of examination results, teachers in elementary schools concentrated their attention, and that of their pupils, on the three Rs to the exclusion of all else. Children learned by heart their reading books during the course of a school year so that when the time came they could recite passages to Inspectors, and in so doing were successful in developing their memory if not their intelligence. Instruction was intended to be both cheap and sound, but in practice whilst it was certainly true that grants to schools were much smaller than previously, a significant rise in the level of literacy did not occur for many years. It is inevitable that progress in the 1870s was hampered by the influx of children who had not hitherto attended school, and for this reason it is not strictly possible to pass judgment on the long term effects of the Code as regards an increase in the level of literacy.

Yet, it would be a mistake to pillory the Revised Code as if in some curious way it was the only obstacle to progress in elementary education. It is not possible for example to forget the unseemly antics of clerics and their opponents prior to 1870 in the struggle for control of education, or the petty, self-defeating rivalries between school boards and voluntary bodies. It is difficult to believe that those who were responsible for drafting the imprecise and contradictory educational and factory legislation after 1870 were really as incompetent as they seemed. This must be considered along with the inconsistency and variability of local byelaws appertaining to school attendance, and the ineffectual penalties which were exacted for absenteeism. Altogether it must be questioned whether there was in fact a tacit acceptance in government, both national and local, that whilst a moderately literate working class was an investment which would yield economic dividends, employers should not be entirely deprived, any sooner than was absolutely necessary, of a cheap source of labour.

In the course of this volume detailed attention has been given to the reading material which was available to children in the Victorian period, both that which was used in schools and that provided for recreational purposes. The content of school books has been criticized at length, and for most of the period the majority of them were found to be technically unsuitable, arid, and uninteresting. Nevertheless, they do not appear to have obstructed the rise in literacy as revealed by the admittedly inconclusive percentage passes in the annual reading examinations. It was possible for teachers to prevent children from entering the examination who were thought unlikely to succeed, and in this way results could be maintained at a highly satisfactory level; but in spite of this it is still evident that a substantial minority of children did not obtain favourable results. Quite apart from the outcome of examinations however, the interest of children in reading could not have been encouraged by the mechanical nature of the alphabetic and phonic methods of teaching as practised at that time, and the unreasoning memorization necessitated by "look and say". The tedious and meaningless repetitions of reading lessons must have effectively stultified any desire on the part of large numbers of children to continue their reading after they had left school, and they were unlikely to pursue an activity which had such unpleasant associations. But this is only part of the truth, for children had access to a wide variety of inexpensive reading material which contained interesting stories, sufficiently brief and uncomplicated to be enjoyed, and which inciden-

172

tally offered the opportunity for them to improve their expertise and raise their level of literacy. Enlightened teachers, clerics, and school boards made available to children books which would arouse their interest and enrich their vocabulary in the form of prizes and school libraries; and towards the end of the century, rate supported public libraries made an increasing contribution to recreational reading and the growth of literacy.

In a study of the influences on literacy in the Victorian period it is sad to reflect that so many of the social and economic factors which could exercise a beneficial effect did not occur until the last decade or more, whilst others were not to be felt until the twentieth century. In the social context, major legislation relating to public health and slum clearance did not become effective until after 1880; and the important amenity of gas lighting was not commonplace in working class h'nes until after 1890. The conflict between educationⱥl and factory legislation was not resolved until the closing years of the century, nor did schools become recognizably attractive, teachers efficient and influential, and local authorities truly mindful of their responsibilities. By 1901 however, so much had been achieved: elementary education had been extended to the vast majority of children and the way was open for the development of secondary education. Before further progress could be made it was imperative for the administration of education to be radically reorganized, for neither the central nor the local administrative machinery were developed to control effectively the expansion which had taken place. A reorganization was partly effected in 1900 when the powers of the principal bodies entrusted with the oversight of instruction were merged in the new Board of Education; and two years later the functions of the school boards were transferred to county, borough, and urban district councils.

It must have appeared to educationists at the commencement of the twentieth century that a state of national literacy could be attained in the foreseeable future, for so much had been done to make this possible in the Victorian period. All that remained, they would have claimed, was to ensure that the literacy of the nation was consolidated and a growth to ever more sophisticated levels encouraged. Those optimists who were

mistakenly persuaded that the coincidence of a new
century and a new reign heralded a new era of
prosperity and cultural achievement, would have
thought it unbelievable that a hundred years after
the Elementary Education Acts, approximately 6% of
the adult population of Britain was either unable
to read or had a literacy level below that of an
average child of nine years of age. They would have
thought it incredible that so many people were not
able to read a daily newspaper, and worse, were
unlikely ever to do so.

Appendices

1862

Standard

I	Narrative in monosyllables.
II	One of the narratives next in order after monosyllables in an elementary reading book used in the school.
III	A short paragraph from an elementary reading book used in the school.
IV	A short paragraph from a more advanced reading book used in the school.
V	A few lines of poetry from a reading book used in the first class of the school.
VI	A short ordinary paragraph in a newspaper or other modern narrative.

> (Committee of Council of Education, Report, 1861-1862, p.xxiii)

1871

Standard

I	One of the narratives next in order after monosyllables in an elementary

reading book used in the school.

II	A short paragraph from an elementary reading book.
III	A short paragraph from a more advanced reading book.
IV	A few lines of poetry or prose.
V	A short ordinary paragraph in a newspaper, or other modern narrative.
VI	To read with fluency and expression.

(Committee of Council on Education,
Report, 1870-1871, p.cix)

1873
Standard

I	A short paragraph from a book used in the school, not confined to words of one syllable.
II	A short paragraph from an elementary reading book.
III	A short paragraph from a more advanced reading book.
IV	A few lines of poetry selected by the Inspector.
V	A short ordinary paragraph in a newspaper, or other modern narrative.
VI	To read with fluency and expression.

(Committee of Council on Education,
Report, 1872-1873, p.lxxxix)

1875
Standard

I	To read a short paragraph from a book not confined to words of one syllable.
II	To read with intelligence a short paragraph from an elementary reading book.
III	To read with intelligence a short paragraph from a more advanced reading book.
IV	To read with intelligence a few lines of poetry selected by the Inspector; and to recite from memory 50 lines of poetry.
V	Improved reading; and recitation of not less than 75 lines of poetry.
VI	Reading with fluency and expression; and recitation of not less than 50 lines of prose, or 100 of poetry.

(Committee of Council on Education,
Report, 1874-1875, p.cxlix)

<u>1879</u> (Amendments to Code of 1875)
Standard
V   Improved reading.
VI   Reading with fluency and expression.

      (Committee of Council on Education,
        <u>Report</u>, 1878-1879, p.373)

<u>1880</u> (Amendments to Codes of 1875 and 1879)
Standard
IV   To read a few lines of prose or poetry
       selected by the Inspector.
V   Improved reading.
VI   Improved reading.

      (Committee of Council on Education,
        <u>Report</u>, 1879-1880, p.119)

<u>1882</u> (Amendments to Codes of 1875 and 1880)
Standard
III   Read a passage from a more advanced
       reading book, or from stories from
       English history.
IV   Read a few lines from a reading book,
       or history of England.
V   Read a passage from some standard
       author, or from a history of England.
VI   Read a passage from one of Shakespeare's
       historical plays or from some other
       standard author, or from a history of
       England.
VII   Read a passage from Shakespeare or
       Milton, or from some other standard
       author, or from a history of England.

      (Committee of Council on Education,
        <u>Report</u>, 1881-1882, p.132)

<u>1890</u> (Amendments to Codes of 1875 and 1882)
Standard
I   To read a short passage from a book not
       confined to words of one syllable.
II   To read a short passage from an
       elementary reading book.
III   To read a passage from a reading book.
IV   To read a passage from a reading book,
       or hsitory of England.

      (Committee of Council on Education,
        <u>Report</u>, 1889-1890, pp.144-5)

APPENDIX II

THE READING EXAMINATION : Results 1864 - 1891

Year	Passes in Reading	Year	Passes in Reading
	%		%
1864	88.13	1878	86.59
1865	88.77	1879	87.53
1866	89.10	1880	88.25
1867	89.77	1881	88.99
1868	90.03	1882	89.22
1869	89.97	1883	89.14
1870	90.89	1884	90.78
1871	88.98	1885	91.86
1872	88.67	1886	92.43
1873	88.64	1887	92.99
1874	88.37	1888	93.45
1875	88.28	1889	94.08
1876	87.09	1890	94.55
1877	85.78	1891	96.87

(Committee of Council on
Education, Reports,
1865-1866 to 1891-1892)

APPENDIX III

SCHEDULE OF LESSON BOOKS FOR THE SCHOLARS
(Reproduced from the Minutes of the
Committee of Council on Education,
Vol.1, 1847-1848, pp.xx-xxvi)

Reading Lesson Books

Educational books -	Society for Promoting Christian Knowledge
The first book	. .
The second book	. .
The third book	. .
Reading Series -	. .
No. 1.	. .
No. 2	. .
Moral and Intellectual Series -	Compiled by some of the chief officers of the British and Foreign School Society

No. 1, Daily lesson
  book
No. 2   ditto   . .
No. 3   ditto   . .
No. 4   ditto   . .
Sequel to No. 1 or
  No. 1 in sheets   . .
Sequel to ditto, No. 2   . .

he Reading Lesson   Compiled and published
Books -   under the authority of
The first   the Commissioners of
The second   National Education in
The third   Ireland
The fourth   . .
The fifth   . .
Sequel to the second   . .
Supplement to the
  fourth   . .
Reading book for the
  use of female schools   . .

irst Reading Book   By the Rev. J.M. McCulloch
econd ditto   . .   LL.D.
hird ditto   . .
eries of lessons in
prose and verse   . .
ourse of elementary
reading   . .

ural Spelling Book   By C.W. Johnson, F.R.S.

he New Series of
chool Books -   Compiled by the Scottish
                           School Book Association
The child's first
  book   . .
o. 1, Primer   . .
o. 2, Second lessons   . .
o. 3, Third ditto   . .
anual of English
  pronunciation; or
  sequel to third
  lessons   . .
heet lessons   . .
o. 4, Readings in
  prose and verse   . .
o. 5, First collection
  of instructive extracts   . .
eprints of vocabularies
  from Nos. 5 and 6   . .

No. 1, Lessons for Schools	the late Rev. A. Thomson D.D.
No. 2, ditto	. .
No. 3, ditto	. .
No. 4, ditto	. .
The Juvenile Reader	By Neil Leitch
Reading Disentangled: being a series of elementary reading lessons on sheets	By the Author of Peep of D

Grammar and Etymology

Manual of English grammar	By the Rev. J.M. McCulloch LL.D
An English grammar for the use of schools	By the Commissioners of National Education in Ireland
Rudiments of English grammar	By A Reid, M.A.
An attempt to simplify English grammar	By Professor R. Sullivan
A system of English grammar	By C.W. Connon
An English grammar	By Allen and Cornwell
Grammar for beginners	By Dr. Cornwell
An initiatory grammar of the English language	By J. Millen
An elementary etymological grammar	By W. Ross
Principles of English grammar	No. 8 of the Scottish Scho Book Association
The young child's grammar	. .
Outlines of etymology	By Rev. A. Wilson
The pupil's guide to English etymology	By G. Manson

Geography

Gecgraphy generalized	By Professor Sullivan
A school geography	By Dr. Cornwell
Compendium of geography	By the Commissioners of National Education in Ireland

180

An introduction to geography and history	By Professor Sullivan
Rudiments of modern geography	By A. Reid, M.A.
Outlines of sacred geography	By A. Reid, M.A.
The young child's geography	No. 9 of the Scottish School Book Association
Outlines of modern geography	No. 10 ditto
Geography of Palestine	By W. M'Leod

English History

A plain and short history of England	By the Bishop of Peterborough
A school history of England	By J.W. Parker

n.b. the schedules for Arithmetic, Mensuration, and Vocal Music have been omitted as not being strictly relevant to the present study.

APPENDIX IV

EXAMPLES OF DIALOGUES IN SCHOOL BOOKS

1   NEIL LEITCH The juvenile reader...
     Glasgow, John Burnett, William Collins. 1839.

Page 54. Extract "On Metals" from Aikin and
         Barbauld's Evenings at home.

George: There are a good many sorts of metals, are
         there not?
Tutor: Yes, thirty eight; and if you have a mind
         I will tell you about the principal ones
         and their uses.
George: Pray do, Sir.
Harry: Yes; I would like to hear it of all things.
Tutor: Well then. First, let us consider what a
         metal is. Do you think you should know
         one from a stone?
George: A stone! - Yes, I could not mistake a
         piece of lead or iron for a stone.
Tutor: How would you distinguish it?
George: A metal is bright and shining.

181

```
Tutor:    True - brilliancy is one of their
          qualities. But, glass and crystal are
          very bright too.
Harry:    But one may see through glass, and not
          through a piece of metal.
```

2   THOMAS DAY   The history of Sandford and Merton
     a book for the young.   1887 edition.
     Thomas Nelson & Sons.   (First pub. 1783/9)

Pages 186-7.

"Harry", said he, "cannot you show your companion
some of the constellations?" - "Yes", answered
Harry, "I believe I remember some, that you have
been so good as to teach me". - "But pray, sir",
said Tommy, "what is a constellation?".

   "Those", answered Mr. Barlow, "who first began
to observe the heavens as you do now, have observe
certain stars, remarkable either for their bright-
ness or position. To these they have given a
particular name, that they might the more easily
know them again, and discourse of them to others;
and these particular clusters of stars, thus joine
together and named, they call constellations. But,
come, Harry, you are a little farmer, and can
certainly point out to us Charles's Wain".

   Harry then looked up to the sky, and pointed out
seven very bright stars towards the North. - "You
are right", said Mr. Barlow; "four of these stars
have put the common people in mind of the four
wheels of a waggon, and the three others of the
horses; therefore they have called them by this
name. Now Tommy, look well at these, and see if
you can find any seven stars in the whole sky, tha
resemble them in their position".

Tommy: Indeed, sir. I do not think I can.
Mr. Barlow: Do you think, then, that you can find
  them again?
Tommy: I will try, sir. Now, I will take my eye of
  and look another way. I protest I cannot find the
  again. Oh! I believe there they are. Pray, sir
  (pointing with his finger), is not that Charles's
  Wain?
Mr. Barlow: You are right; and, by remembering
  these stars, you may very easily observe those
  which are next to them, and learn their names too
  till you are acquainted with the whole face of th
  heavens.
Tommy: That is indeed very clever and very

surprising. I will show my mother Charles's Wain,
the first time I go home; I dare say she has
never observed it.
Mr. Barlow: But look on the two stars which
compose the hinder wheel of the waggon, and raise
your eye up towards the top of the sky: do you
not see a very bright star, that seems to be
almost, but not quite, in line with the two
others?
Tommy: Yes, sir; I see it plainly.
Mr. Barlow: That is called the Pole-star; it never
moves from its place, and by looking full at it,
you may always find the North.
Tommy: Then, if I turn my face toward that star, I
always look to the North.
Mr. Barlow: You are right...

3 MARY GODOLPHIN Sandford and Merton in words of
   one syllable. Cassell, Petter, and Galpin.
   1872 (?).

Pages 142-4.(The same example as that in the
original in words of one syllable.)

"Can you not tell Tom the names of the groups of
stars, Hal?"
Hal: Not all of them, I fear, sir.
Mr. Barlow: Come, Hal, as you were brought up at a
farm, I think you can at least point out to us
Charles's Wain.
So Hal bade Tom look at five bright stars, and
three more a short way off.
Mr. Barlow: The four stars are like the wheels of
a cart, and the rest are like the horse that draws
the cart. Now, Tom, look well at them, and see if
you can find a group of stars that are like them
as to the way they stand.
Tom: No, sir, I do not think I can.
Mr. Barlow: Now look on the two stars which stand
for the hind wheels of the cart, and raise your
eyes straight up. Do you not see a bright star
that seems to be but is not quite, on a line with
them?
Tom: Yes, sir, I do.
Mr. Barlow: That is the Pole Star; it does not stir
from its place, and if you look full at it, you
may find the north.
Tom: Then if I turn my face to that star I look to
the north?
Mr. Barlow: You are right.

EXAMPLES OF BABY TALK, WORKING CLASS ACCENTS, AND
BROKEN ENGLISH IN VICTORIAN CHILDREN'S BOOKS

Carroll, Lewis, <u>Sylvie and Bruno</u>(Macmillan:1889),
pp.307-8.

"What's the matter, darling?" said Sylvie, with
her arms round his neck.
"Hurted mine self welly much!" sobbed the poor
little fellow.
"I am so sorry, darling! How did you manage to
hurt yourself so?".
"Course I managed it!" said Bruno, laughing
through his tears. "Doos oo think nobody else but
oo ca'n't manage things?".
Matters were looking distinctly brighter, now
Bruno had begun to argue. "Come, let's hear all
about it!" I said.
"My foot took it into its head to slip -" Bruno
began.
"A foot hasn't got a head!" Sylvie put in, but all
in vain.
"I slipted down the bank. And I tripted over a
stone. And the stone hurted my foot! And I trod on
a Bee. And the Bee stinged my finger!". Poor Bruno
sobbed again. The complete list of woes was too
much for his feelings.
"And it knew I didn't <u>mean</u> to trod on it!" he
added, as the climax.

Ballantyne, R.M., <u>The lighthouse</u>(James Nisbet:1865)
p.3.

"D'ye see the breakers noo, Davy?" inquired the
ill-favoured man, who pulled the aft oar.
"Aye, and hear them too", said Davy Spink, ceasing
to row, and looking over his shoulder towards the
seaward horizon.
"Yer een and lugs are better than mine, then",
returned the ill-favoured comrade, who answered,
when among his friends, to the name of Big Swankie.
"Od! I believe ye're right", he added, shading his
heavy red brows with his heavier and redder hand,
"that <u>is</u> the rock, but a man wad need the een o' an
eagle to see onything in the face o' sik a bleezin'
sun. Pull awa', Davy, we'll hae time to catch a bit
cod or a haddy afore the rock's bare".

MacDonald, George, <u>At the back of the North Wind</u>
  (First published 1871, Blackie edition. 1886),
  p.183.

"Wife", said the cabman, turning towards the bed,
"I do somehow believe that wur a angel just gone.
Did you see him, wife? He warn't werry big, and he
hadn't got none o' them wingses, you know. It wur
one o' them baby-angels you sees on the grave-
stones you know".
  "Nonsense, hubby!" said his wife; "but its just
as good. I might say better, for you can ketch hold
of <u>him</u> when you like. That's little Diamond as
everybody knows, and a duck o' diamonds he is! No
woman could wish for a better child than he".
  "I ha' heerd on him in the stable, but I never see
the brat afore. Come, old girl, let bygones be
bygones, and gie us a kiss, and we'll go to bed".

Ballantyne, R.M., The dog Crusoe: a story of
  adventure in the western prairies(First published
  1861,Thomas Nelson:1869), pp.108-9, 117.

"He's a 'cute chap that", remarked Joe, with a
sarcastic smile; "I dont feel quite easy about
gettin' away. He'll bother the life out o' us to
get all the goods we've got, and, ye see, as we've
other tribes to visit, we must give away as little
as we can here".
  "Ha! you is right", said Henri; "dat fellow's eyes
twinkle at de knives and tings like two stars".
  "Fire-flies, ye should say. Stars are too soft an'
beautiful to compare to the eyes o' yon savage",
said Dick, laughing...

  "Ye may be thankful yer neck's whole", said Joe,
grinning, as Henri rubbed his shoulder with a
rueful look. "An' we'll have to send that Injun and
his family a knife and some beads to make up for
the fright they got".
  "Hah! an' fat is to be give to me for my broke
shoulder?".
  "Credit, man, credit", said Dick Varley, laughing.
  "Credit! fat is dat?".
  "Honour and glory, lad, and the praises of them
savages".
  "Ha! de praise? more probeebale de ill-vill of de
rascale. I seed dem scowl at me not ver' pritty".
  "That's true, Henri, but sick as it is it's all
ye'll git".

APPENDIX VI

EXAMPLES OF GRAMMATICAL DEFECTS IN EPHEMERAL AND
PERIODICAL LITERATURE

1 THE BOY'S OWN PAPER, No.1, Vol.1, Saturday,
   January 18, 1879.

Page 10.(Extract from From powder monkey to
admiral, by W.H.G. Kingston.)

Bill's mother was buried in a rough shell by the
parish, and Bill went out into the world to seek
his fortune. He took to curious ways; hunting in
dust-heaps for anything worth having; running
errands when he could get any one to send him;
holding horses for gentlemen, but that was not
often; doing duty as a link-boy at houses when
grand parties were going forward or during foggy
weather; for Bill, though he often went supperless
to his nest, either under a market-cart, or in a
cask by the river-side, or in some other out-of-
the-way place, generally managed to have a little
capital with which to buy a link, but the said
capital did not grow much, for bad times coming
swallowed it all up.

2 CHAPBOOK LITERATURE

The famous history of Valentine & Orson. Glasgow.
   c.1820. Pages 14-15.

Now Orson was resolved to set him free, or lose
his life in the attempt; and putting on the arms
of a dead Saracen, he called Pacolet: so both of
them went through the enemy's army, without being
discovered, till they arrived at the tent where the
duke was confined, the guards of which were cast
into a deep sleep by Pacolet: which done, they took
off the duke's chains, and giving him a horse, he
rode back to the Christian army; who when they
beheld their Duke at liberty, cried out - Long live
the Duke of Aquitain! The Saracens were so sore
dismayed, that they fled in great confusion, when
the Christians followed them, till night forced
them to return into the city, but not till they had
scarce left Ferragus a thousand men, of all the
numerous army he brought with him, against the Duke
of Aquitain: being obliged to return into Portugal,
with the disgrace of being beat with a small army
of Christians.

The history of Whittington and his cat. York,
J. Kendrew. c.1820. Pages 5-7.

Dick Whittington was so very young when his father
and mother died, that he neither knew them nor the
place of his birth. He strolled about the country,
as ragged as a colt, till he met with a waggoner
who was going to London, and he gave him leave to
walk by the side of his waggon, without paying
anything for his passage, which obliged little
Dick very much, having heard that the streets were
paved with gold, he was willing to get a little of
it; but great was his disappointment, when he saw
the streets covered with dirt instead of gold, and
himself in a strange place, without food, friends,
or money. Though the waggoner was so charitable as
to let him walk by the side of his waggon gratis,
he took care not to know him when he came to town,
and the poor boy was in a little time so cold and
hungry that he wished himself at a good kitchen
fire in the country...

The history of Wat Tyler and Jack Straw. Warrington.
c.1810. Pages 4-5.

In the beginning of the King's reign, the French on
the one side, and the Scots on the other, cruelly
infested this land until John Philpot, Citizen and
Alderman of London, lamenting the misery of the
times, occasioned by the neglect of securing the
coast, and scouring the seas whereby the merchant
durst not traffic abroad for fear of pirates, who
hovered in every corner; but especially one Mercer,
a Scottish Rover, who had got together a great
fleet of French, Scotch, and Spaniards, and with
them did rob all they met, and did a great deal of
mischief, complained thereof to the King's council,
acquainting them with the daily wrongs sustained
by the sail Mercer; imploring their aid; but
receiving from them no relief, he at his own cost
fitted out a fleet of ships and went with them
himself to sea; and in a short time took the said
Mercer, and recovered all the prizes which he had
formerly taken, with fifteen Spanish bottoms, well
laden with riches, besides many French and Scotch
ships; for which brave action he incurred the
dislike of most of the noblemen, from whom they
thought he seemed to have by this harduous and
fortunate attempt, the native cognizance of true
nobility.

Boys'-Weekly-Reader Novelette

No. 12, Vol.2, Page 14, (Extract from The Black Buccaneer.)

He began by asking the girl her name, and she told him that it was Umnandi(sweet flower).

"And a very appropriate name too", said Tom, "But why should a sweet flower be so sad?"

He had some little difficulty in gaining her confidence at first, but at last he elicited from her that she was loved by and returned the love of a youth of her tribe called Umkonka, or the stag; as however he had never slain a foe, he was not allowed to marry; and so, having arrived at marriageable age, fifteen, the chief had commanded her to wed a middle-aged warrior called Utangafola, who already had three wives.

"And why, since he loves you so much, doesn't Umkonka go and kill a foe?" asked Tom.

"Because we haven't been at war for three years, and then Umkonka was too young", was the reply.

"But if you cannot marry Umkonka, I suppose you can refuse to wed Utangafola?" queried our hero.

"Not unless I prefer being burnt alive..."

"Confound it!" he ejaculated a minute later, "why, what's that?"

He had brushed something off his face that tickled consumedly; and well it might, with such numerous appliances for the purpose, for when Tom looked down on the ground to see what it was that he had knocked off him, he descried a great, ten or eleven inch long, hairy, many-jointed, hundred-legged thing, that he at once knew to be an African centipede.

"By George!" he muttered, "if that chap has bitten me I'm gone soon and no mistake".

"No, no", exclaimed the native maiden excitedly. "Umnandi suck wound an' poison come all out. Massa bit sleepy perhaps but well as ebber again bime bye. You just stoop down lillie bit".

"Oh, no, Umnandi; I couldn't allow you to undertake such a dangerous and unpleasant task".

"Dangemrous, not at all. Poison no hurt in um mouth, an' spit he out besides to make quite sure. As to suck cheek, what harm dat?"

"Forgive me!" cried Joe Chambers, falling upon his knees, and raising his hands. "I was very poor - very poor, and - and after all I did not commit murder".

"No, sure enough", replied Percy gravely, "You did not. It was fortunate for you you did not, for murder would have been brought to light as sure as this crime has. I am acquainted with all the particulars. In my pocket is the confession of a man who has been dead some time. I don't know whether you have heard of him, but he also was mixed up in it".

"Who was that, sir?"

"A man who I always thought was my father".

"John Follard?" cried Joe.

"Yes, the same".

"Good heaven! he is dead, you say?"

"He is".

"Then, replied Joe, as he raised his hand, "your chance of getting the estates is gone".

"I say no. I have his confession in my pocket; and if you will do as I tell you, you will be of service. Will you do as I tell you?"

"With all my heart and soul; if you will trust me I will do just what you tell me, but sir - "

"Well?"

"Where is - where - "

Joe stopped abruptly.

"Say on and fear not".

"Ah, you don't recollect," said Joe sadly.

"Recollect what?".

"You had a sister"...

APPENDIX VII

SCHOOL LIBRARY STATISTICS

	School Libraries in England and Wales	Elementary Day Schools Inspected in England and Wales
1880	2,092	17,614
1881	2,382	18,062
1882	2,603	18,289
1883	3,046	18,540
1884	3,322	18,761

1885	3,589	18,895
1886	3,842	19,022
1887	4,056	19,154
1888	4,142	19,221
1889	4,311	19,310
1890	4,401	19,419
1891	4,967	19,508
1892	5,560	19,515
1893	5,832	19,577
1894	6,225	19,709
1895	6,381	19,739
1896	6,550	19,848
1897	7,066	19,958
1898	7,398	19,937
1899	7,875	20,064
1900	8,114	20,100
1901	8,272	20,116

(Committee of Council on Education, Reports,
1880-1881 to 1898-1899; Board of Education,
Reports, 1899-1900 to 1901-1902)

Bibliography

OFFICIAL PUBLICATIONS

The Statutes of the United Kingdom of Great
  Britain and Ireland, etc. 1833-1899:

1833(3 & 4 William 4), ch.103. Labour of children,
                                 etc. in Factories
                                 Act.
1834(4 & 5 William 4), ch.76. Poor Law Amendment
                                 Act.
1844(7 & 8 Victoria), ch.15.   Factories Act.
1847(10 & 11 Victoria), ch.29. Factories Act.
1850(13 & 14 Victoria), ch.54. Factories Act.
1850(13 & 14 Victoria), ch.65. Public Libraries Act.
1855(18 & 19 Victoria), ch.70. Public Libraries Act.
1864(27 & 28 Victoria), ch.48. Factories Acts Ext-
                                 ension Act.
1867(30 & 31 Victoria), ch.103.Factories Act Ext-
                                 ension Act.
1867(30 & 31 Victoria), ch.130.Agricultural Gangs
                                 Act.
1870(33 & 34 Victoria), ch.75. Elementary Education
                                 Act.
1873(36 & 37 Victoria), ch.67. Agricultural Child-
                                 ren Act.
1874(37 & 38 Victoria), ch.44. Factory Act.

1876(39 & 40 Victoria), ch.79. Elementary Education
                                Act.
1878(41 & 42 Victoria), ch.16. Factory and Work-
                                shop Act.
1880(43 & 44 Victoria), ch.23. Elementary Education
                                Act.
1891(54 & 55 Victoria), ch.56. Elementary Education
                                Act.
1891(56 & 57 Victoria), ch.75. Factory and Work-
                                shop Act.
1892(55 & 56 Victoria), ch.53. Public Libraries
                                Act.
1893(56 & 57 Victoria), ch.42. Elementary Education
                                (Blind and Deaf
                                Children)Act.
1893(56 & 57 Victoria), ch.51. Elementary Education
                                (School Attendance)
                                Act.
1899(62 & 63 Victoria), ch.13. Elementary Education
                                (School Attendance)
                                Act 1893, Amendment
                                Act.
1899(62 & 63 Victoria), ch.32. Elementary Education
                                (Defective and Epi-
                                leptic Children)
                                Act.

Board of Education, Consultative Committee on Books
    in Public Elementary Schools, Report, 1928.
Board of Education, Reports, 1899-1913.
Census of England and Wales, 1871, General Report,
    1873; 1901, Preliminary Report, 1901; 1901,
    General Report, 1904.
Census of Great Britain, 1851, Population Tables,
    Vol.1, 1852.
Children's Employment Commission, First Report,
    1842; Second Report, 1843; Fifth Report, 1866.
Committee of Council on Education, Minutes and
    Reports, 1839-1899.
Departmental Committee on the Pupil Teacher System,
    Report, 1898.
Elementary Education Acts, England and Wales,
    Minutes of Evidence, 1886 and 1887; Final Report,
    1888.
Elementary Schools, Dr. J. Crichton-Browne's
    Report to the Education Department upon the
    Alleged Over-Pressure of Work in Public
    Elementary Schools, 1884.
Registrar General of Births, Deaths, and Marriages
    in England, Annual Report, 1898.

Royal Commission on Scientific Instruction and the
Advancement of Science, First, Supplementary,
and Second Report, 1872.
Royal Commission on Secondary Education, Report,
9 volumes, 1895.
Royal Commission on the Blind, the Deaf and Dumb,
etc.of the United Kingdom, Report, 1889.
Schools Inquiry Commission, Report, 21 volumes,
1868.
Select Committee on Education, Minutes of Evidence,
1835.
Select Committee on Public Libraries, Minutes of
Evidence, 1849; Report, 1849.
The State of Popular Education in England, Report,
6 volumes, 1861.
Training Colleges, Report, 1899.

BOOKS AND MANUSCRIPTS

Adamson, J.W., The Illiterate Anglo-S,xon,
Cambridge University Press, 1946.
Allen, W.O.B. and McClure, E., Two Hundred Years:
the history of the S.P.C.K., 1698-1898, Society
for Promoting Christian Knowledge, 1898.
Altick, R.D., The English Common Reader: a social
history of the mass reading public, 1800-1900,
University of Chicago Press, 1957.
Anonymous, Boys and Their Ways: a book for and
about boys, John Hogg, 1880
Arnold, M., Reports on Elementary Schools, 1852-
1882, Macmillan, 1889.
Avery, G., Childhood's Pattern: a study of the
heroes and heroines of children's fiction,
1770-1950, Hodder and Stoughton, 1975.
Bain, A., Education as a Science, 5th ed., Kegan,
Paul, Trench, 1885.
Banks, J.A., Prosperity and Parenthood: a study of
family planning among the Victorian middle
classes, Routledge and Kegan Paul, 1954.
Banks, J.A. and O., Feminism and Family Planning
in Victorian England, University of Liverpool
Press, 1964.
Barnett, P.A., Common Sense in Education and
Teaching: an introduction to practice, Longmans,
Green, 1899.
Bingham, J.H., The Period of the Sheffield School
Board, J.W. Northend, 1949.
Binns, H.B., A Century of Education: being the
centenary of the British and Foreign School
Society, 1808-1908, J.M. Dent, 1908.

Birchenough, C., History of Elementary Education in England and Wales from 1800, University Tutorial Press, 1914.

Booth, C.(ed), Labour and Life of the People, 2 volumes, Williams and Norgate, 1891.

Brereton, J.L., County Education: a letter addressed to the Right Hon. Earl Fortescue, James Ridgway, 1856.

Briggs, A., The Age of Improvement, 1783-1867, Longmans, 1959.

Brown, C.K.F., The Church's Part in Education, 1833-1941, National Society, 1942.

Buxton, S., Over-Pressure in Elementary Education, Swan, Sonnenschien, 1885.

Calderwood, H., On Teaching: its ends and means, 4th ed., Macmillan, 1885.

Carter, T., Life and Letters, ed. by W.H. Hutchings, Longmans, Green, 1903.

Chadwick, E., Report on the Sanitary Condition of the Labouring Population of Great Britain, First published 1842, edited by M.W. Flinn, University of Edinburgh Press.

Chambers, W. and R., (eds), Infant Education: from two to six years of age, Chambers, 1852.

Christian, G.A., English Education from Within, Wallace Gandy, 1922.

Church, R., Over the Bridge, Heinemann, 1955.

Clarke, W.K.L., A History of the S.P.C.K., Society for Promoting Christian Knowledge, 1959.

Cole, G.D.H. and Postgate, R., The Common People, 1746-1938, 4th. ed., Methuen, 1968.

Credland, W.R., The Manchester Public Free Libraries, Manchester Public Libraries, 1899.

Cruickshank, M., Church and State in English Education, 1870 to the Present Day, Macmillan, 1963.

Currie, J., The Principles and Practice of Common-School Education, James Gordon, 1862.

Curtis, S.J., An Introductory History of English Education Since 1800, 4th ed., University Tutorial Press, 1966.

Curwen, H., A History of Booksellers: the old and the new, Chatto and Windus, 1873.

Dale, N., Further Notes on the Teaching of English Reading, George Philip, 1902.

Dale, N., On the Teaching of English Reading, 2nd. ed., J.M. Dent, 1903.

Darton, F.J.H., Children's Books in England, 3rd. ed., Cambridge University Press, 1982.

dwards, E., _Free Town Libraries: their formation, management and history_, Trübner, 1869.

goff, S.A., _Children's Periodicals of the Nineteenth Century_, Library Association, 1951.

llis, A.C.O., _Books in Victorian Elementary Schools_, Library Association, 1971.

llis, A.C.O., _A History of Children's Reading and Literature_, Pergamon, 1968.

llis, A.C.O., _Library Services for Young People in England and Wales, 1830-1970_, Pergamon, 1971.

ngels, F., _The Condition of the Working Class in England_, First published 1844, Translated and edited by W.O. Henderson and W.H. Chaloner, Basil Blackwell, 1958.

he _English Catalogue of Books_, 5 volumes and Supplements, Sampson Low, Son and Marston, 1835-1900.

nsor, R.C.K., _England, 1870-1914_, Oxford University Press, 1936.

ield, Mrs. L.F., _The Child and His Book: some account of the history and progress of children's literature in England_, 2nd ed., Wells Gardner, Darton, 1892.

itch, J.G., _Lectures on Teaching_, Cambridge University Press, 1881.

ill, J., _Introductory Text Book to School Education, Method and School Management_, New ed., Longmans, Green, 1882.

ladman, F.J., _School Work: organization and principles of education_, Jarrold, 1885.

ordon, P. and Lawton, D., _Curriculum Change in the Nineteenth and Twentieth Centuries_, Hodder and Stoughton, 1978.

reenwood, T., _Public Libraries_, 3rd ed., Simpkin Marshall, 1890; 4th ed., Simpkin Marshall, 1894.

reenwood, T., _Sunday-school and Village Libraries_, James Clarke, 1892.

reenwood, T., (ed), _Greenwood's Library Year Book_, 1897; Cassell, 1897; 1900-1901, Scott, Greenwood, 1901.

ewitt, G., _Let the People Read: a short history of the United Society for Christian Literature_, United Society for Christian Literature, 1949.

orn, P., _Education in Rural England, 1800-1914_, Gill and Macmillan, 1978.

utchins, B.L. and Harrison, A., _A History of Factory Legislation_, 3rd ed., P.S. King, 1951.

uxley, T.H., _Science and Education_, Macmillan, 1893.

nternational Health Exhibition, _Literature_, 19

volumes, William Clowes, 1884.

Kay, J., The Social Condition and Education of the People in England and Europe, 2 volumes, Longman Brown, Green, and Longmans, 1850.

Kay-Shuttleworth, J.P., Public Education, Longman Brown, Green, and Longmans, 1853.

Kay-Shuttleworth, J.P., Social Problems, Longmans Green, 1873.

Keeling, F., Child Labour in the United Kingdom: a study of the development and administration of the law relating to the employment of children, P.S. King, 1914.

Kelly, T., A History of Public Libraries in Great Britain, 1845-1965, Library Association, 1973.

Knight, C.(ed), London, 2 volumes, Charles Knight 1851.

Landon, J., School Management, 7th ed., Kegan Paul Trench, 1889.

Laurie, S.S., Primary Instruction in Its Relation to Education, 4th ed., James Thin, 1890.

Library Association, Monthly Notes, 4 volumes, 1880-1883.

Liverpool, Benevolent Society and Free School of St. Patrick, Committee Book, 1831-1872.

Liverpool, St. Columba's Mixed School, Diary, 1866-1894.

McLean, R., Victorian Book Design and Colour Printing, Faber and Faber, 1963.

Manchester Statistical Society, Report on the State of Education in the Borough of Liverpool, 1835-1836, James Ridgway, 1836.

Mayhew, H., London Labour and the London Poor, 3 volumes, Charles Griffin, 1850.

Miall, L.C., Thirty Years of Teaching, Macmillan, 1897.

Midwinter, E.C., Victorian Social Reform, Longmans 1968.

Minto, J., A History of the Public Library Movement in Great Britain and Ireland, Allen and Unwin, 1932.

Mitchell, B.R. and Deane, P., Abstract of British Historical Statistics, Cambridge University Press, 1962.

Money, L.G.C., Riches and Poverty, Methuen, 1905.

Morley, J., The Struggle for National Education, 2nd ed., Chapman and Hall, 1873.

Moyle, D., The Teaching of Reading, 4th ed., Ward Lock, 1976.

Muir, P.H., English Children's Books, 1600 to 1900 Batsford, 1954.

196

unford, W.A., _Penny Rate: aspects of British public library history, 1850-1950_, Library Association, 1951.

usgrave, P.W., _Society and Education in England Since 1800_, Methuen, 1968.

orris, J.P., _The Education of the People: our weak points and our strength_, Thomas Laurie, 1869.

'Dea, W.T., _The Social History of Lighting_, Routledge and Kegan Paul, 1958.

gle, J.J., _The Free Library: its history and present condition_, George Allen, 1897.

erkin, H., _The Origins of Modern English Society, 1770-1880_, Routledge and Kegan Paul, 1969.

orter, G.R., _The Progress of the Nation_, New ed., Methuen, 1912.

atcliff, C., _Ragged Schools in Relation to the Government Grants for Education_, Longman, Green, Longman, and Roberts, 1861.

eid, H., _The Principles of Education: an elementary treatise_, Longman, Brown, Green, and Longmans, 1854.

ich, R.W., _The Training of Teachers in England and Wales During the Nineteenth Century_, Cambridge University Press, 1933.

obins, S., _Twenty Reasons for Accepting the Revised Educational Code_, Longman, Green, Longmans and Roberts, 1862.

obson, A.H., _The Education of Children Engaged in Industry in England, 1833-1876_, Kegan Paul, 1931.

owntree, B.S., _Poverty: a study of town life_, Macmillan, 1901.

owse, A.L., _A Cornish Childhood_, Cape, 1942.

unciman, J., _Schools and Scholars_, Chatto and Windus, 1887.

almon, E., _Juvenile Literature As It Is_, H.J. Drane, 1888.

ampson, H., _A History of Advertising_, Chatto and Windus, 1874.

eaborne, M., _The English School: its architecture and organization, 1370-1970_, 2 volumes, Routledge and Kegan Paul, 1971 and 1977.

enior, N.W., _Suggestions in Popular Education_, John Murray, 1861.

ilver, H., _Education and History: interpreting nineteenth and twentieth century education_, Methuen, 1983.

palding, T.A., _The Work of the London School Board_, P.S. King, 1900.

turt, M., _The Education of the People: a history of primary education in England and Wales in the

Nineteenth Century, Routledge and Kegan Paul, 1967.

Sunday School Society for Ireland, Hints for Conducting Su ay Schools, 1835.

Taine, H., Notes on England, First published 1869, Translated by Edward Hyams, Thames and Hudson, 1957.

Thwaite, M.F., From Primer to Pleasure in Reading an introduction to the history of children's books in England from the invention of printing to 1914, 2nd ed., Library Association, 1972.

Townsend, J.R., Written for Children: an outline of English-language children's literature, 2nd revised ed., Kestrel Books, 1983.

Traill, H.D. (ed), Social England, 6 volumes, Cassell, 1893-1897.

Tremenheere, H.S., I Was There: the memoirs of H.S. Tremenheere, Edited by E.L. and O.P. Edmonds, Shakespeare Head Press, 1965.

Trevelyan, G.M., British History in the 19th Century and After, 1782-1919, New ed., Longmans, Green, 1937.

Watts, J., The Facts of the Cotton Famine, Simpkin Marshall, 1866.

Waugh, E., Home Life of the Lancashire Factory Folk During the Cotton Famine, Manchester Examiner, 1867.

Wiggin, K.D., Children's Rights: a book of nursery logic, Gay and Hancock, 1892.

Williams, E., George: an early autobiography, Hamish Hamilton, 1961.

Wolff, R.L., The Golden Key: a study of the fiction of George MacDonald, Yale University Press, 1961.

PERIODICALS AND PERIODICAL ARTICLES

Anonymous, 'The Fonetic Solution for Hard Names', Punch, 16(1849), p.84.

Anonymous, 'The Spell-Bound Enthusiasts', Punch, 15(1848), p.250.

Anonymous, 'A Visit to a Training College', Monthl Packet, 14(1872), pp.397-9.

Bailey, T.J., 'The Planning and Construction of Board Schools', Royal Institute of British Architects Journal, 6(1899), pp.405-32.

Chambers's Edinburgh Journal, 1844-1900.

Collins, W., 'The Unknown Public', Household Words 18(1858), pp.217-222.

Fuller, S.D., 'Penny Dinners', Contemporary Review, 49(1885), pp.424-32.

Library, Volumes 1-10, 1889-1899
Library Association, Transactions and Proceedings
  of the Annual Meeting, 1878-1879.
Library Association Record, Volumes 1-52, 1899-
  1950.
Library Chronicle, Volumes 1-5, 1884-1888.
Millar, J.H.,'Penny Fiction',Blackwood's Magazine,
  164(1898), pp.801-11.
Nineteenth Century, Volumes, 1-50, 1877-1901.
Quarterly Review, Volumes 71-191, 1842-1900.
Stone, L., 'Literacy and Education in England',
  1640-1900, Past and Present, No.42, February
  1969, pp.69-139.
Webb, R.K.,'Working Class Readers in Early Victorian England', English Historical Review,
  65(1950), pp.333-51.
White, G., 'Children's Books and Their Illustrators', The Studio, Special Winter Number,
  1897-1898, pp.3-68.
Yonge, C.M.,'Children's Literature of the Last
  Century', Macmillan's Magazine, July 1869,
  pp.229-37; August 1869, pp.302-310; September
  1869, pp.449-56.

SCHOOL BOOKS

Anonymous, Cassell's Modern School Series. First
  Reader, Cassell, 1885.
Anonymous, The Holborn Series of Reading Books,
  New Reader, Book I, Educational Supply Assoc-
  iation, c.1884.
Commissioners of National Education in Ireland,
  Second Book of Lessons for the Use of Schools,
  1855.
Day, T., The History of Sandford and Merton: a book
  for the young, Stockdale, 1783-89; Nelson, 1887.
Godolphin, M., Sandford and Merton in Words of One
  Syllable, Cassell, Petter, and Galpin, c.1872.
Harris's First Book, Reading Made Completely Easy,
  Otley, J.S. Publishing and Stationery, c.1870.
Heywood, J.(ed), Manchester Readers: a new series
  for elementary schools of all grades, The
  Primer and The First Book, Manchester, John
  Heywood, 1871.
Laurie, J.S., Standard Series, The Third 'Standard'
  Reader, stories of animals; The Fourth 'Standard'
  Reader, fables and parables, John Marshall,
  c.1871.
Leitch, N., The Juvenile Reader, Glasgow, John
  Burnet and William Collins, 1839.
Meiklejohn, J.M.D., The Golden Primer, 2 Parts,

Blackwood, 1884.

Mogridge, G., The New Illustrated Primer,
S.W. Partridge, 1870.

Mortimer, Mrs. F.L., Reading Without Tears; or, a
Pleasant Mode of Learning to Read, Thomas
Hatchard, 1857.

Religious Tract Society, The Little Learner's Toy
Book, 1876.

Society for Promoting Christian Knowledge, First
Reading Book, Parts 3 and 4, 1854.

Society for Promoting Christian Knowledge, Reading
Book, Standard III, c.1871.

Tait, S.B., Jarrold's Empire Readers, Jarrold,
c.1885.

CHILDREN'S RECREATIONAL LITERATURE
1. Books and Chapbooks

Aikin, J. and Barbauld, A.L., Evenings at Home,
London, 1792-1796.

Anonymous, The Famous History of Valentine and
Orson, Glasgow, c.1820.

Anonymous, The History of Wat Tyler and Jack Straw,
Warrington, c.1810

Anonymous, The History of Dick Whittington and His
Cat, York, John Kendrew, c.1820.

Ballantyne, R.M., The Dog Crusoe, Nelson, 1861.

Ballantyne, R.M., The Lighthouse, J. Nisbet, 1865.

Carroll, L., Sylvie and Bruno, Macmillan, 1889.

Ewing, J.H., Jackanapes, S.P.C.K., 1884.

Ewing, J.H., Six to Sixteen, Bell, 1875.

Henty, G.A., Under Drake's Flag, Blackie, 1883.

Henty, G.A., With Wolfe in Canada, Blackie, 1887.

Kingsley, C., The Water Babies, Macmillan, 1863.

MacDonald, G., At the Back of the North Wind,
Strahan, 1871.

Marryat, F., Masterman Ready, Longmans, 1841.

Marryat, F., Mr. Midshipman Easy, Saunders and
Otley, 1836.

Marryat, F., Settlers in Canada, Longmans, 1844.

Molesworth, M.L., Carrots: just a little boy,
Macmillan, 1876.

Ruskin, J., The King of the Golden River, Smith and
Elder, 1851.

Trimmer, S.K., The History of the Robins, Longmans,
1786.

2. Periodicals

Boys of England, 1866-1899.
The Boy's Own Paper, 1879-1967.
Boys'-Weekly-Reader Novelette, 1881-1883.

Index

Shakespeare, W. 53, 98, 136
Sheffield 63, 70, 76, 83, 152
Sherwood, Mrs. M. 128, 130, 132, 145
Shropshire 34
Sickness 7-8, 37
Simpkin Marshall 105, 114
Simultaneous instruction 87
Sinclair, C. 128
Skilled workers 9, 10, 170
Smallpox 14
Smith, W.H. 137
Society for Promoting Christian Knowledge 104, 106, 110, 112, 113, 121, 130, 131, 132, 135, 139, 141 143, 149, 154, 157
Somerset 43
Spalding, T.A. 70
Spedding, J. 91
Staffordshire 34, 35, 83
Standard of living, see Living standards
Stevenson, R.L. 128, 129, 131, 163
Stipendiary monitors 44
Stockport 11
Stoke Newington 162
Stowe, H.B. 131, 140, 141
Sunday school libraries see Libraries: Sunday school
Sunday School Union 158
Sunday schools 19, 41, 132
Surveys of reading, see Reading: surveys
Swan Sonnenschien 130
Swift, J. 128, 134
Taine, H. 11
Taunton 20

Taunton Commission (1868) 24
Teacher training colleges 23, 46-60, 87 see also under individual colleges
Teaching profession 20, 49-50, 58-60
Tegg, T. 130, 140
Tenniel, Sir J. 143
Textbooks, see School books
Textile industry 3-4, 8, 20, 30
Times, The 136
Tit-Bits 136
Trade unions 10
Training colleges, see Teacher training colleges
Tremenheere, H.S. 33, 137, 153, 156
Trimmer, Mrs. S.K. 113, 114, 127, 131, 145
Tuberculosis 14
Twain, M. 141
Typhus fever 14
Unemployment 5, 10
Uninspected schools 22
Untrained teachers 42, 58
Uxbridge 159
Vaccination 14, 37
Ventilation 7, 14, 68, 69, 70, 80
Verne, J. 130, 134, 141
Vocabulary 144-6
Voluntary schools 19, 20, 22, 24, 36, 68, 71, 122, 151, 171
Voluntary Schools Act (1897) 62
Wages
  Teachers 60-62
  Other 4, 8, 30, 32, 44, 170
Walton, Mrs. O.F. 132
Warburton, Canon 56
Warrington College 55, 57